NORMANDY

DIE WEHRMACHT IM KAMPF

NORMANDY

From Cotentin to Falaise, June–July 1944

FRIEDRICH HAYN

Translated by
LINDEN LYONS

Series editor:
MATTHIAS STROHN

CASEMATE
Pennsylvania & Yorkshire

AN AUSA BOOK
Association of the United States Army
2425 Wilson Boulevard, Arlington, Virginia, 22201, USA

This edition first published in the United States of America and Great Britain in 2022
Reprinted as a paperback in 2025 by
CASEMATE PUBLISHERS
1950 Lawrence Road, Havertown, PA 19083, USA
and
47 Church Street, Barnsley, S70 2AS, UK

© 2022 Association of the U.S. Army
English translation © 2022 Casemate Publishers

Introduction © Matthias Strohn

Originally published as Die Wehrmacht im Kampf Band 2: Friedrich Hayn, *Die Invasion: Von Cotentin bis Falaise* (Heidelburg: Scharnhorst Buchkameradschaft der Soldaten, 1954)

Publisher's note: This text is a faithful translation of the original German and as such includes some language that is now considered offensive.

Paperback Edition: ISBN 978-1-63624-533-1
Digital Edition: ISBN 978-1-63624-157-9

A CIP record for this book is available from the British Library

All rights reserved. No part of this book may be reproduced or transmitted in any form or by any means, electronic or mechanical including photocopying, recording or by any information storage and retrieval system, without permission from the publisher in writing.

Printed and bound in the United Kingdom by CPI Group (UK) Ltd, Croydon, CR0 4YY
Typeset in India by Lapiz Digital Services, Chennai.

For a complete list of Casemate titles, please contact:

CASEMATE PUBLISHERS (US)
Telephone (610) 853-9131
Fax (610) 853-9146
Email: casemate@casematepublishers.com
www.casematepublishers.com

CASEMATE PUBLISHERS (UK)
Telephone (0)1226 734350
Email: casemate@casemateuk.com
www.casemateuk.com

Front cover image: One of the 210 mm guns of the German Crisbecq Battery in Normandy, not far away from Utah Beach, June 1944. (U.S. Coast Guard. Office of Public and International Affairs)

The Publisher's authorised representative in the EU for product safety is Authorised Rep Compliance Ltd., Ground Floor, 71 Lower Baggot Street, Dublin D02 P593, Ireland.
http://www.arccompliance.com

Contents

Foreword by Matthias Strohn   vii
Introduction   xi

1 The first day (6 June 1944)   1
2 The battle of Cherbourg (7–26 June 1944)   33
3 The breakthrough of the Americans (26 June–31 July 1944)   65
4 The Falaise pocket   93
5 The last days in Normandy (18–21 August 1944)   121
6 General observations   133
7 The daily activities of military intelligence   149
    Formations mentioned in the text   161

References   167
Index   169

Foreword

The battle of Normandy is one of the most iconic clashes of arms of World War II. In the western world, it is often seen as the defining battle (or rather operation) of the most total war the world has ever seen. This book covers the fighting of the German LXXXIV Army Corps in France from the D-Day landings on 6 June 1944 until the end of the Falaise pocket, concentrating to a certain degree on the fighting against the US forces. The author, the former Major Friedrich Hayn, was the chief of the intelligence section (the Ic in German military language at the time) of the headquarters of the LXXXIV Army Corps during the period that this book covers. Although Hayn provides detailed descriptions of the fighting in this book, his task during the battle was not to participate actively in the fighting, but to provide the corps with information and intelligence about the enemy. Hayn makes clear that the intelligence work had been neglected by the German Wehrmacht and he vividly describes the problems that intelligence officers such as him faced. It is in this area that the book offers the most interesting insights into the German fighting in Normandy.

The original German version of the book was published in 1954 and was the second volume of the *Wehrmacht im Kampf* series. Directly after the war, German publications were predominantly memoirs by former high-ranking officers. Their writings were, inevitably, subjective and often characterised by the attempt to put all blame of the defeat on Hitler. In order to evaluate the military experience more objectively, the *Wehrmacht im Kampf* series was started, which continued to publish books until 1974. Most of the studies were written by former staff officers, and the writing style generally reflects this. It is objective, and by concentrating on matters relating to staff work and the decisions taken by staffs it can appear detached from the suffering of the soldiers. Not all volumes can stand up to more modern historical scrutiny. The events were too raw, many of the writers had been personally involved, and hardly any source material was available, often with the exception of those files held by individuals. This also shines through in this book; for instance, the author mentions Paul Hausser, a Generaloberst of the Waffen SS. Hayn describes him as a good soldier and a man of honour, but he fails to mention the war crimes that Hausser's units committed during the war. And yet, the series offers fascinating insights into the minds of the former actors and their analysis of the events that they often had lived through personally. The books are also an indicator of the developing Cold War and the attempt to prepare the German Bundeswehr and its new NATO allies for a conventional war against the Warsaw Pact. The book that you, the reader, hold in your hands, follows the general approach of the series outlined above.

Based on his experiences and intelligence analysis Hayn formed a very clear picture of the combat effectiveness of the US troops. He never fails to point out the low morale of the US troops and contrasts it with the high morale of the Germans and their effectiveness in the field of battle. He also argues that the Allied soldiers were less liked by the local population than the Germans (something that I found, at least partially, confirmed during conversations with locals in Normandy during numerous staff rides). While this provides an interesting juxtaposition to the general understanding of the battle of Normandy, which too often seems to have been informed by Hollywood movies, he does take all of this too far. The text makes one wonder whether Hayn actually realised that the Germans had lost the battle for Normandy and, subsequently, the war. It is not beyond the realm of possibility that he adopted these views to help him cope with the personal suffering caused by the war. As he points out in the introduction, he had lost both his sons. From the context we can deduce that they were killed in action in 1945 during the closing stages of the war and that both were approximately 18 years of age at the time of their deaths.

If placed correctly into the modern historical narrative, this book still offers many valuable insights into the fighting in Normandy from the German perspective, in particular in the area of intelligence, which today, just as in 1944, seems often neglected. It is for these reasons that this book is recommended to you, the reader.

Prof. Matthias Strohn, M.St., DPhil., FRHistS
Head of Historical Analysis, Centre for Historical Analysis and Conflict Research, Camberley
Visiting Professor of Military Studies, University of Buckingham

Introduction

This book deals with the decisive first few weeks of the invasion of Normandy in 1944. It therefore covers an important, perhaps even the most important, part of World War II. As was the case with Stalingrad in 1943, Falaise was the tragic turning point for an entire front.

Events are described from the point of view of the chief of the intelligence section of the headquarters of the LXXXIV Army Corps. The book details how the fighting unfolded – mainly against the Americans – and how it came to be that our troops were defeated. It serves also as a commemorative volume for our old comrades in the army corps, and especially for those who fell on the battlefield. Their fate may be overshadowed by the events, yet it was those very men who played a role in shaping those events.

I dedicate this book to the brave soldiers on both sides and to those who sacrificed themselves in battle. I dedicate it to my two sons, Dieter and Hartmuth, both born in 1927. Dieter was declared missing in action near Potsdam, while Hartmuth was killed in action at Fortress Courbière in Graudenz. Many parents likewise lost their sons in the war, so this book is dedicated to them as well.

Several fellow combatants are deserving of my warm thanks. They read this work in whole or in part, provided me access to unpublished reports or accounts, and offered valuable help and criticism. I thank General of Panzer Troops Heinrich Eberbach, Lieutenant-General Paul Mahlmann, Major-General Rudolf-Christoph Freiherr von Gersdorff, Colonel Wilhelm Meyer-Detring, Lieutenant-Colonel Friedrich von Criegern, Lieutenant-Colonel Günther Keil, and Captain Wilhelm Ritter von Schramm.

Bordesholm, Holstein, on 6 June 1954
Friedrich Hayn

Map 1: France on 6 June 1944

CHAPTER I

The first day (6 June 1944)

It was Monday 5 June 1944. Towards 2200 hours, several waves of aircraft belonging to the Allied air forces appeared over the eastern coast of the Cotentin Peninsula in Normandy. When the clock of the Cathedral of Saint-Lô struck midnight, three officers of the headquarters of the LXXXIV Army Corps entered the main room of the bunker in the city. Those officers were Lieutenant-Colonel Friedrich von Criegern, Major Hasso Viebig, and Major Friedrich Hayn. The commander of the army corps, General of Artillery Erich Marcks, glanced up in surprise as they entered. It was his birthday, born as he had been on 6 June 1891. He was averse to any sort of celebration. His gaunt face, with its disciplined features, could have been that of a teacher. The prosthetic leg he had had worn since the early days of the campaign in Russia creaked as he stood up. The wave of his hand was both friendly and cool. Everyone stood and drank a glass of Chablis, and then the celebration was over only a few minutes after it had begun.

The general leant over the two situation maps that Major Hayn, his third general staff officer, had laid out in front of him. He wanted to examine them in preparation for the conference that was scheduled to take place in Rennes that morning between all the divisional and corps commanders of the Seventh Army. The first map showed the distribution of Allied forces in southern England, with more than 30 enemy divisions marked on it. In the east was the Canadian sector, in the centre the British, and in the west the American. Highlighted were five airborne divisions. Deep in thought, the general studied the coloured flags, the red and blue lines and arcs, the shaded ovals, and the overlapping districts.

The second map showed the development of the situation in the air over the course of the preceding few months. It displayed most clearly what had already been known for a long time: the gradual and systematic Anglo-American success in establishing air supremacy. The operational bombing offensive that had been conducted by the enemy since May 1943 had damaged the air industry in the Fatherland, had been detrimental to the production of synthetic fuel, and had inflicted heavy losses on the German fighter defences. The map highlighted the state of paralysis of the French railway network, especially along the railway line that connected Hamm, Maastricht, Amiens, Rouen, Caen, and Cherbourg. This was the main supply line for the entire coastal front, but the enemy had also destroyed other railway lines, like that which ran via Metz and Bar-le-Duc. Traffic in and around Paris had come to a halt, for Allied bombers had struck the railway yards on the outskirts of the city. Even small road bridges on the Seine between Paris and Rouen and on the Loire between Orléans and Nantes had been destroyed. It was clearly the intention of the enemy to isolate the area occupied by the Seventh Army and to disrupt the flow of supplies to that area.

The tactical measures of the enemy air forces in the combat zone of the army corps were shown in red. Allied objectives increasingly lay near the coast. These included gun emplacements, radar installations like Observation Post Ginsterhöhe in La Pernelle, V-1 launch facilities south of Cherbourg that were still under construction, and various strongpoints that were likewise still to be completed. There had recently been daily reports of low-level flights over the beaches. Flying almost at sea level, the enemy aircraft were presumably photographing our underwater obstacles and our main line of resistance. Some of these aircraft were shot down by corps artillery and others by the defensive weaponry near railway branch lines in the rear area of the army corps. But this was only small consolation for the disruption of the traffic system, the overstraining of the repair and maintenance units, and the erosion of the morale of the men and of the French population.

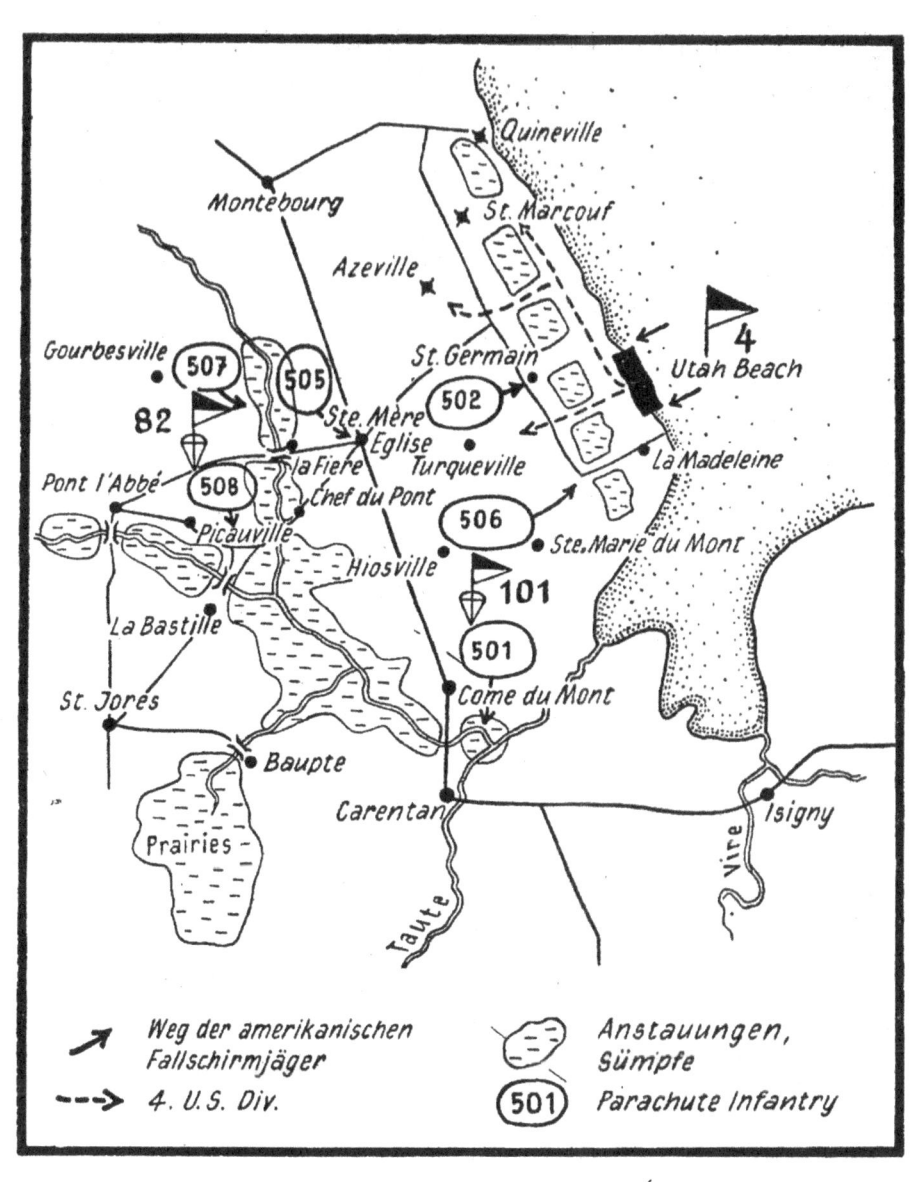

Map 2: The landing site at Sainte-Mère-Église

Most noteworthy was the extensive aerial reconnaissance carried out by the Royal Air Force (RAF) and the United States Army Air Forces (USAAF) on the evening of 4 June 1944. Countless condensation trails had stretched across the blue skies above Normandy.

General Marcks requested the special maps of our artillery positions, sea defences, and minefields, and he also asked for the map of the freshwater dams of the Aure, Douve, and Merderet Rivers near the Isigny–Carentan sector. But at 0111 hours – a time easily remembered – the field telephone rang. It was soon apparent that this was an important call. The general straightened up as he listened, while his right hand gripped the edge of the table. With a head movement, he indicated to his chief of staff to listen in. The caller reported: 'Enemy paratroopers have landed to the east of the mouth of the Orne. The main combat area lies between Bréville and Ranville and on the northern side of the Bois de Bavent. Counter-measures are underway.' This news from the 716th Infantry Division struck the headquarters of the LXXXIV Army Corps like a bombshell.

Was this finally *the invasion*, the assault on Fortress Europe? Someone suggested hesitantly: 'Maybe they are no more than strong liaison detachments assigned to support the forces of the French Resistance? What do you think, Ic?' The third general staff officer responded: 'The parachute landings have taken place too close to our main line of resistance for them to be able to reinforce, or indeed revive, the French Forces of the Interior in the sector of our army corps. It would require a fundamental change in the situation in the rear area for the enemy to try to do such a thing. The slow yet amiable peasants of Normandy have thus far refused to engage in acts of sabotage.'

It was a different situation in the neighbouring sector to the west, on the fiercely contested ground of Brittany. The day before, in the vicinity of Saint-Malo, leaflets with mysterious announcements were distributed by hand or thrown into letterboxes: '*La carotte rouge est quittée.*' In addition, our radio operators had picked up an unusually large number of coded messages. The resistance groups had hitherto been careful to avoid any sort of overt hostility. They were aware of the danger of being discovered and annihilated.

While the parachute landings in the combat zone of the 716th Infantry Division were still being discussed, a report arrived from the 709th Infantry Division in Valognes: 'Enemy paratroopers have appeared to the south of Saint-Germain-de-Varreville and in the vicinity of Sainte-Marie-du-Mont. A second group has touched down to the west of the Carentan–Valognes road, specifically on either side of the Merderet along the road connecting Sainte-Mère-Église and Pont-l'Abbé. There is fighting for control of the crossings.' By then it was 0145 hours.

   Three airborne landings near the front! Two of them clearly lay near important crossings that were needed to relieve our traffic jams. The third sealed off the marshy meadows near the mouth of the Dives and the bridge over the canalised Orne at Ranville. This area was where the boundary of the army corps lay. It was a natural flank for the army corps and would most certainly serve as one for the enemy should he succeed in establishing a foothold there. The task of the paratroopers was to seize tactically important landmarks from the air and to hold on to them until the ground troops, or more specifically the seaborne landing troops, fought their way through to them and absorbed them into the main front line. On top of that, the paratroopers would be able to paralyse our coastal defences in Normandy by attacking the strongpoints that lay immediately to the west of the beach. If it was indeed the objective of the reported enemy forces to take and hold on to the crossings, then it could be expected that seaborne landings would take place soon. This was without question a serious situation!

   The third general staff officer saw to it that the French postal communication network was shut down immediately. Reports soon arrived from the units of the army corps that prisoners had been taken. It was ascertained that the British 3rd Parachute Brigade (of the British 6th Airborne Division) had landed near Caen. In the meantime, the paratroopers that had appeared in the combat zone of our 709th Infantry Division were Americans. The southern group was the US 101st Airborne Division (with the 501st and 506th Parachute Infantry Regiments) and the northern the US 82nd Airborne Division (with the 505th Parachute Infantry Regiment). This meant that approximately 75 per cent of the parachute and airborne units that we had previously identified in southern England were now committed to action in Normandy. The enemy sought a decisive outcome to the war by conducting an invasion across the English Channel.

Seaborne landings had yet to occur. If they did so in the early hours of the morning, the German defences were prepared. It is true that we could not know on which day the invasion would begin, so it was quite possible that we might be taken by surprise. We had been unable to conduct thorough aerial reconnaissance over the southern coast of England for a long time; our aircraft could not penetrate the enemy anti-aircraft defences. If we had been able to constantly observe the river mouths and hiding places of the coast in any weather, we could have kept track of the progress of the assembly of enemy ships and landing craft. We fumbled around in the dark when it came to obtaining information on Allied preparations and could only rely on the occasional spy reports of cancellations of leave and so on. The statements that had been made by a member of the French Resistance who had been arrested towards the end of May had not been taken seriously. Only the extensive aerial reconnaissance conducted by the enemy on 4 June rang alarm bells.

The choice of the day of the invasion was dependent on a number of factors that had to coincide. The enemy would be able to exploit his aerial superiority most effectively if he made use of the entire day, something that was particularly important given that time would be needed for the transportation of troops across the Channel. A night when the moon was full would provide illumination and thus make both airborne and seaborne landings easier. Good weather, with neither cloud cover nor fog, would mean good visibility for enemy bombers. Finally, it was desirable from the point of view of the enemy that the landings be scheduled while the tide was coming in so that his troops could land further forward, enabling them to identify obstacles quickly and avoid being exposed in the open for too long.

Several of these factors coincided at the beginning of June. However, our weather forecasters had predicted severe conditions at sea for 6 June, so it did not seem as if a seaborne landing would be likely that day. Wanting to take advantage of this moment of reduced danger, the headquarters of the Seventh Army ordered that all its corps and divisional commanders partake in a wargame in Rennes on the morning of 6 June. In addition, Field Marshal Erwin Rommel, the commander of Army Group B, was on his way to attend a conference in Obersalzberg. The official view seemed to be that no invasion had taken place in May and that because of this something of the kind could hardly occur before August. The result was that the most important field commanders were scheduled to be away on the very morning they would be needed at the front.

The command post of the army corps resembled a beehive. The constant toing and froing between being on standby and being ready for action had come to an end. The troops had been kept on their toes since the middle of April, but they were inured to it by early June and no longer took the measures of their superiors seriously. However, the Allied bombardment was now cause for alarm!

Messages were sent in all directions as a matter of high priority. The divisional commanders who were still at their command posts had to remain where they were. Those who had already departed for Rennes needed to return immediately. Most divisional commanders reported their presence: Lieutenant-Generals Dietrich Kraiß, Rudolf Graf von Schmettow, Wilhelm Richter, and Heinz Hellmich. Only Lieutenant-General Karl-Wilhelm von Schlieben and Major-General Wilhelm Falley were absent. The former had already left on the late afternoon of 5 June, for the distance he would have to cover from his headquarters at Château de Chiffrevast, near Valognes, to the location of the planned conference in Rennes amounted to 190 kilometres. The following message was delivered to him at his hotel at 0630 hours on 6 June by an orderly officer of the garrison headquarters in Rennes: 'The wargames have been cancelled. Commanders must return to their units immediately.' Shortly thereafter, another officer informed him that an invasion had been underway for five hours. The commander of our 91st Air Landing Division, Major-General Wilhelm Falley, had heard the considerable noise of vehicle motors and air raids while on his way to Rennes and had told his driver to turn around. The driver raced along the roads through the departments of Ille-et-Vilaine and Manche, bringing the major-general straight towards his death. The headquarters of the air landing division at Château de Bernaville, north of Picauville, had already been occupied by the Americans by the time Falley jumped out of the car in the courtyard. A few shots were fired, and he and his driver were dead. He had not had an opportunity to issue a single order. Soon afterwards, the American group there, which belonged to the 508th Parachute Infantry Regiment, was destroyed, and the divisional command post once more came under German control. Major-General Falley was buried in the gardens behind the main building, and he was succeeded by one of his regimental commanders, Colonel Eugen König, a recipient of the Knight's Cross of the Iron Cross with Oak Leaves.

Reports came one after the other from dawn onwards. General Marcks sent a status report to the Seventh Army at 0400 hours, after which he ordered the unit in army corps reserve, the 915th Infantry Regiment (of the 352nd Infantry Division), to head towards Carentan. Our counter-attacks in the vicinity of Caen commenced at 0500 hours, with the objective of retaking the bridge that connected Bénouville and Ranville over the Orne and the Canal de Caen à la Mer and that had fallen intact into the hands of the British. By that stage, there had been no contact for half an hour with Army Field Gun Battery Merville, which lay on the east bank of the mouth of the river.

The following report was received at 0530 hours: 'Sudden bombardment of our strongpoints along the coast of Calvados by heavy naval artillery.' At the same time, the Luftwaffe signal centre in Caen announced the approach of large formations of enemy aircraft. Control towers, radar installations, and various positions were hit hard. The whitish-grey smoke thrown into the air by the explosions stretched across the horizon like enormous floating mushrooms. Our communication network was in a state of chaos. This was especially the case for the shallowly laid earth system between companies and battalions. Unfortunately, it was precisely these smaller units whose reports needed to reach the military leadership if a clear picture of the situation was to be gained.

The enemy committed more than one thousand bombers to action at the crack of dawn. It was his intention to weaken our line of strongpoints along the beaches so significantly that his seaborne assault troops would be spared the need to overcome formidable defences.

And then it was H-Hour. The first general staff officer of the army corps read aloud the following report: 'Landings in the combat zone of the 352nd Infantry Division on the coast of Calvados between Vierville and Colleville at 0630 hours.' Further landings took place at 0700 hours and 0730 hours. The first of these was to the north-east of Carentan, at La Grande Dune, and the second on the right wing of the army corps, between Port-en-Bessin and Riva-Bella. These times corresponded to the flood tides at each beach. Subsequent reports revealed that further attack waves followed the first at each beach at intervals of half an hour. It was 0930 hours by the time there was a reasonable degree of clarity as to what was happening. Landings were taking place to the north of the bay outside Carentan, with the enemy troops assaulting the line of strongpoints (nos. 2a to 10) in the sector of the 919th Infantry Regiment (commanded by Lieutenant-Colonel Günther Keil). Strongpoint 5, manned by the 3rd Company (Lieutenant Arthur Janke) of the 919th Infantry Regiment, was the first to experience major contact with the enemy. The troops of the company were buried in rubble and later dug up by the Americans.

In Saint-Lô, the bunker of the headquarters of the army corps rumbled ominously as heavy bombs fell on the city. Like Valognes, Périers, and Tessy-sur-Vire, the city of Saint-Lô was the location of an important road junction. Enemy aircraft conducted carpet bombing so that the rubble of houses would block the roads to the greatest extent possible. Although the population was advised in a number of broadcasted announcements to flee to the country, hundreds of civilians were nevertheless buried beneath the debris. A beautiful cityscape with its medieval half-timbered buildings was razed to the ground.

The minutes crept by. It was a nerve-racking situation. Reports came in quickly: some of them matched one another in their accounts, while others were contradictory. The headquarters of the Seventh Army and that of Army Group B telephoned constantly. For now, the headquarters of the LXXXIV Army Corps could do nothing but wait until some sense could be made of the overall situation, for confusion still reigned. A clearer idea needed to be gained of the focal points of the airborne and seaborne landings. Further reports were needed from our strongpoints so that we could know which ones still stood and which ones had fallen. Reports from reconnaissance units and statements from prisoners of war would also be valuable. All the reports that were received came only from army units. The Luftwaffe could have helped to clarify the situation, but it was nowhere to be seen. Although there were a number of facts and small pieces of information that had reached the army corps, they were insufficient to piece together a good picture of the overall situation. What could be ascertained were the approximate locations of the three landing zones. It was fortunate that many of the most important communication cables continued to work for a while. They had been laid deep under the ground and were therefore mostly unaffected by all the carpet bombing. For approximately 10 days, telephone communications were maintained with the German headquarters in Valognes and with that in Cherbourg, even though many of the villages through which the cables ran were occupied by the enemy in the meantime.

Fate had thrown the LXXXIV Army Corps a curve ball. It was the main formation that stood in the way of the Allied onslaught. At this point, it is worth having a closer look at its leadership.

General of Artillery Erich Marcks possessed one of the finest minds in the Wehrmacht. He was a clear thinker, with both the sharp objectivity of a general staff officer and the conscientiousness of a researcher. His development of the operational plan for the campaign in Russia in 1941 was a demonstration of his brilliancy. He was regarded by many military figures as having great potential for leadership at the most senior level. He allowed those under his command considerable intellectual freedom. His personal frugality bordered on asceticism.

The son of the professor and historian Erich Marcks, the young Erich Marcks occupied himself not only with the vigorous work required of a professional soldier but also with the study of art and science. Many a treatise came from his pen. Even during times of war, his cultural awareness, his sense of humanity, and his reverence for history never waned. He was the chief of staff of Georg von Küchler's Eighteenth Army during the campaign in France in 1940. He kept the combat zone away from the beautiful medieval city of Bruges in Flanders, and 14 days later, on 13 June 1940, he spared the bridges over the Seine in

Paris from bombardment and thereby avoided the destruction of the city centre.

He lost a leg during the campaign in Russia, suffering severe eye and head injuries at the same time. He remained a keen rider despite the need for a prosthetic limb. Attending unit exercises and visiting strongpoints and batteries daily, he simply slid down inclines on his stump. Woe betide anyone who offered him help! Always triumphing over his physical disability, he was greatly admired by officers and men. Everyone in the army corps was convinced that the outcome of the fighting would be favourable under his leadership.

Hitler prevented Marcks from reaching a top leadership position. The general had been a former ministerial director in the cabinet of Kurt von Schleicher and was therefore regarded as 'politically unacceptable'. When, in 1943, he was earmarked for the command of a field army in Italy and had already made his way as far as Avignon, he was recalled. General of Infantry Rudolf Schmundt, who was both the chief adjutant of the Wehrmacht and the chief of the army personnel office, spoke to General Marcks confidentially on 1 August 1943 and had the following to say: 'The unexpected change in the situation in Italy might require that the high-ranking commanders assigned there take a political stance or some sort of action against Italian Fascism. Upon making his decision, the Führer considered it a requirement that generals who have been politically prominent in the past should not be appointed. Although he recognises the sacrifices you have made for the Fatherland, he has rejected the proposal to post you in Italy under the current circumstances.' General Marcks therefore had to endure what many of our best minds had to after 1933. He was often considered an ideal candidate whenever an important post needed to be filled, and, driven by his concern for what increasingly seemed to be the imminent fate of the German Army and thus of the German people, he would have carried out his task to the best of his ability. However, he always ended up being excluded from such posts. He overcame these setbacks with an unlimited and very Prussian devotion to the performance of his duties. Life dealt him many severe blows: he was constantly worried about a daughter who had fallen ill, and he grieved for two sons who had fallen on the battlefield. He often brooded over the meaning of existence, and those who worked closely with him regarded him as one of the finest representatives of humanity. Nobody under his command was deprived of the experience of the warmth of his personality.

The chief of staff of the army corps was Lieutenant-Colonel Friedrich von Criegern, who stood out with his calm objectivity and precise knowledge of all tactical matters. The burden of responsibility weighed heavily on him, which was necessary so that his commander could focus fully on leading the army corps. The chief of staff remained a valued helper in all situations. He was able to increase the efficiency with which the general performed his duties and thereby enabled him to combine good judgement with quick decision-making. This was especially important in those critical days of June 1944. As a teacher of military theory and as a soldier with experience from multiple theatres of war, Criegern was highly capable. He was always fit for action and, as one of the best skiers in the army, was a participant in many sporting competitions.

The remaining hours of the morning of 6 June went by slowly. Everyone was consumed by the worrying question as to whether the weeks and even months of work put into preparing our defences would pay dividends. Such preparations included the dispersal of coastal barracks and the construction of foreshore obstacles designed to counter the enemy special vehicles we were aware of, like the Landing Craft Tank (LCT), the Landing Craft Assault (LCA), the Landing Craft Motor (LCM), and the Landing Craft Flak (LCF). We also prepared 'asparagus fields', which were areas where thousands of tree trunks had been rammed into the ground for the purpose of impeding enemy airborne landings. The tree trunks were connected by barbed wire, and many of them were also mined. Every single trunk appeared to sit at the centre of a spider's web that lay in wait for military gliders. Pits were dug so that paratroopers would fall into them and find it difficult to move. Much help was provided by the French people in the preparation of these fields. Although paid well, they were glad to help! They hoped that such measures would keep their farms and home villages from becoming sites of battle zones.

At 1015 hours, important details were provided over the telephone by the 352nd Infantry Division. The troops and the divisional headquarters had responded quickly to the bombardment. The third general staff officer of the infantry division, a man who combined great skill with tremendous luck and zeal, informed us that the American prisoners that had been taken in the central sector of the seaborne landings at Saint-Laurent-sur-Mer belonged to the 116th Infantry Regiment (of the US 29th Infantry Division), the 5th Ranger Battalion (also of the US 29th Infantry Division), and the 16th Infantry Regiment (of the US 1st Infantry Division).

Due to low cloud cover, enemy bombers had not quite been able to strike German strongpoints in the combat zone of the 352nd Infantry Division. The smoke over the coast and the light morning mist even blocked the view of the artillerymen on board an enemy battlecruiser. Many landing boats were shot to pieces or capsized in the surging waves, and most of their occupants were drowned and washed away. Some of them clung on for dear life to the steel crosses of our underwater obstacles and were laboriously pulled ashore with lifelines whilst subjected to barrage fire. The Americans experienced the greatest difficulties in unloading their tanks and heavy weaponry. Most of the enemy troops had to wade through extensive stretches of water whose waves reached chest height.

Despite having suffered heavy casualties and being too exhausted to regroup, the enemy troops lunged towards the fully intact German bunkers. Smoke had concealed the bunkers before then. Although they were occupied only by a reinforced battalion of the 914th Infantry Regiment (Colonel Ernst Goth), they blocked many of the gradually ascending access routes that led to higher ground. The attack waves sought temporary cover in blind spots at the foot of steep cliffs, but this meant that they made slow progress and suffered further bloodshed. The US 116th Infantry Regiment lost half its combat strength as it struggled forward. Enemy sources later declared that the US 29th Infantry Division lost 1,500 men on 6 June. The US 1st Infantry Division lost 30 per cent of its combat strength. In order to reduce visibility for the German defenders, the landing vehicles fired incendiary shells into the dry midsummer grass. The resulting thick smoke lasted well into the afternoon. Nevertheless, the Americans held only a narrow sector and

14 • NORMANDY

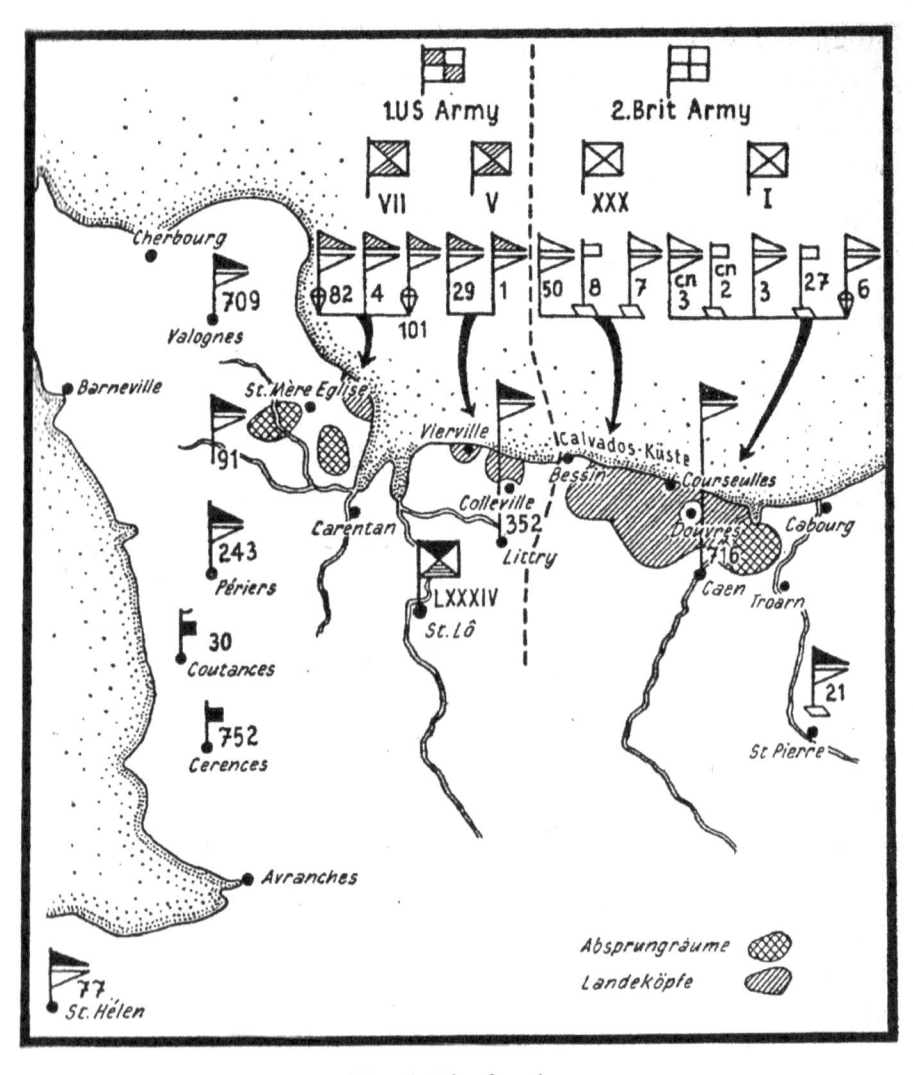

Map 3: The first day

were unable to move for the time being. So paralysing were their losses that even further waves of seaborne landings could do nothing to give impetus to the attack. It was a critical situation. Small numbers of enemy troops eventually climbed the cliffs and infiltrated the German defensive line at points on the high ground where it had become wafer-thin. They carefully circled the stationary strongpoints, and some of them pushed as far as the roads that would be needed for the effective employment of the tanks that were on their way.

By 1800 hours, the Americans had achieved a depth of penetration of between 2 and 4 kilometres at several points along the German main line of resistance. There were no German reserves in this sector of the front, for the army corps had already detached the 915th Infantry Regiment and sent it to the Carentan area. The Americans made use of new special equipment such as tracked vehicles capable of driving over beach obstacles and damaged roads, and there were also flail vehicles designed to cut through minefields. Large parts of the mined areas had in any case already been detonated by the hail of bombs and shells.

The first prisoners taken by the army corps had fallen from the skies and belonged to the US 82nd Airborne Division (commanded by Major General Matthew Ridgway). These prisoners were without exception physically strong and had been well-equipped. Depending on their temperament, they gazed at their interpreters anxiously, curiously, or, in most cases and despite their hidden irritation, calmly. The first four prisoners that were taken immediately created an impression of the nature of the composition of their formation. There was an officer of Anglo-Saxon descent with red hair. He was downcast: 'My glider crashed. I spent the night in a wet bush in the company of a cow that looked at me pityingly.' There was a Pole with a shaved head and fanatical features who had narrowly avoided capture in 1939. A half-breed from California with Mongolian characteristics carried a pass that identified his 'race' as 'coloured'. The last man was someone by the name of Braun, born in Stuttgart in 1913, and he awkwardly tried to conceal his origins. His family had emigrated in 1929, and he spoke German fluently. The 82nd Airborne Division truly honoured its nickname 'All American'. America, the great melting pot!

The questioning revealed little regarding the tactical situation, but it did, in conjunction with various reports and intercepted radio messages, give us a vivid picture of the state of the airborne division immediately after its troops had jumped. Specifically, its situation was anything but good. Heavy cloud cover and strong gales caused the military gliders to touch down too far away from one another. The area they covered was approximately 25 or 30 kilometres in width. An important objective for the paratroopers was to seize the crossings over the freshwater dams of the Merderet, especially the road connecting Sainte-Mère-Église and Pont-l'Abbé, but it turned out that many of the paratroopers landed in the flood area itself. The US 507th Parachute Infantry Regiment landed right in the middle of water that, due to the thickly growing grass that emerged above its surface, had appeared to be meadow from the air. The men of the parachute infantry regiment, burdened with heavy equipment, often found themselves chest-deep in water and could barely move, let alone assemble. The wounded drowned. Many a tragedy unfolded silently. Valuable military gliders were lost, along with men and materiel. Although the average depth of the swamps was only one metre, there were a number of particularly dangerous crisscrossing drainage ditches whose depth was roughly two metres. With the forces of the airborne division split by the almost impassable Merderet, the American leadership lost control of the situation.

The airborne division was soon embroiled in costly fighting when German forces belonging to our 91st Air Landing Division and 6th Parachute Regiment scoured the terrain around the swamps in the early hours of the morning. The odds were stacked against the American paratroopers: the weather, the water, the scattered airborne landings, the minefields, and the German preparatory positions. Despite its years of training, the airborne division suffered such heavy casualties that it was nearly wiped out. Its troops often wandered into minefields, either in the darkness or in attempting to avoid our forces. They soon had to be reinforced through the arrival of further companies by air. Small groups of enemy troops remained isolated for several days; it was best to draw as little attention to themselves as possible during that time.

Yet the enemy situation varied. He who was lucky landed on a dry, unoccupied spot and remained undisturbed. Here and there a platoon could assemble without being shot at. It must be remembered that our rear area was only lightly occupied, so it was not unusual for the Americans to come across reserve units of no more than eight to 10 men. In such cases, the Americans succeeded in their efforts to capture strongpoints or fortified houses. Other enemy groups proved incapable of reaching their objectives or retaking ground they had temporarily held and lost. The US 505th Parachute Infantry Regiment took up a position of all-round defence in Sainte-Mère-Église, which had been given up by a German flak unit, and waited anxiously for the arrival of the US 4th Infantry Division, which had landed on the beaches.

The US 101st Airborne Division fared somewhat better, although it still lost more than 30 per cent of its personnel and more than 60 per cent of its equipment as it landed en masse between the coast and the dams at 0130 hours. Most of those losses were simply the result of accidents. We were aware of this thanks to the hastily sent radio messages we intercepted. Subordinate commanders called for reinforcements, ammunition, rations, and medical supplies. Several of the modern Waco and Horsa II military gliders had been dashed to pieces upon touching down. They had struck tree trunks and large branches in the airborne landing area, filled as it was with hedges and fruit trees. Many more gliders had tipped forwards in the narrow gullies that were to be found everywhere.

These crash-landings meant that many of the troops on board were killed or wounded. Those that could move scattered and formed only small groups. Although they used ratchets, the noise of which resembled the chirping of crickets, and 'magic balls' [magischen Kugeln], which, instead of the animal calls used by the Germans, were an acoustic and visual aid for the assembly of troops, only 10 or 20 or at most 30 men came together in the darkness. These groups were not large enough to act as spearheads. Many of them marched to the east so as to establish contact with the troops that had arrived by sea. They were lucky that we failed to execute immediate counter-thrusts. The length of coast defended by the German 919th Infantry Regiment amounted to approximately 30 kilometres. Such an extensive front would ordinarily have been covered by three full-strength divisions! Furthermore, the aerial and naval bombardment conducted by the enemy had had a detrimental effect on the German garrisons. By dawn, most of our troops were pinned to their strongpoints.

The American paratroopers frequently demonstrated little fighting spirit. The situation they encountered upon their arrival in Normandy appeared a hopeless one. They were split up into small groups and surrounded, lacking the necessary strength to clear and expand the areas they held. Their inability to fight under the strongly observed principle of 'safety first' had a significant impact on morale. An example of this phenomenon is the fighting at the strongpoint of the 13th Company of our 919th Infantry Regiment at Saint-Germain-de-Varreville. The company comprised almost 50 men and was armed with four Russian 7.35cm howitzers. Although the enemy had spotted the strongpoint and had bombarded it with his shipboard guns, he had been unable to destroy it. Almost without a fight, scouting parties from the strongpoint brought in more than their own number of prisoners. Since no one could take the disarmed Americans away, they were kept in groups of various sizes between the defenders all day long. An American medical orderly was entrusted with looking after the wounded.

Although the fighting dissipated here and there into dozens of smaller skirmishes, the struggle for important crossings or major strongpoints remained fierce. At no stage that day did the guns fall silent. It was late afternoon by the time we, with great effort, ascertained where the enemy forces had ensconced themselves. We neither identified nor exploited the weaknesses of the Americans quickly enough. Much depended on whether what was left of the six or more enemy airborne regiments and other enemy formations could soon be supported by artillery arriving from the sea. The airborne forces would be finished if such support did not materialise. According to the calculations made later by the US VII Corps, the total losses of the 82nd and 101st Airborne Divisions from 6 June to 1 July 1944 amounted to 1,600 dead, 4,500 missing, and 3,700 wounded. Most of those losses occurred in the first couple of days.

The situation at 1300 hours was summarised in a status report prepared by the LXXXIV Army Corps:

> The enemy forces in the British sector have made progress in the vicinity of Caen, while those in the eastern part of the American sector have been repelled at Vierville. Our counter-attacks near Sainte-Mère-Église have succeeded in tying down the US 8th Infantry Regiment (Colonel James Van Fleet) of the US 4th Infantry Division. Where is our aerial support? Enemy aircraft are disrupting our supply lines and all our movements by day.

This was a reasonably favourable assessment of the situation. The enemy airborne troops in the vicinity to the south of Montebourg had been pushed back. It was possible that the US 4th Infantry Division, a well-known elite formation, might try to intervene, but it was for the time being stuck on the beach in a small 3-kilometre sector.

In the British sector of the seaborne landings, the command post of our 21st Panzer Division in Saint-Pierre-sur-Dives, which lay approximately 24 kilometres south-east of Caen, had already received the order at 0630 hours to move its forces into their assembly areas. Lieutenant-General Edgar Feuchtinger was to conduct a counter-thrust at the critical moment of any landing, namely after the first wave had landed and had suffered casualties. However, already to be seen was what the enemy would so often exploit in future: the interference by the Green Table of the Führer Headquarters in far distant East Prussia, not only in operational conduct but also in tactical details.

General Marcks did not manage to have a panzer formation placed at his immediate disposal. Though usually quite calm, he spoke ever more heatedly with the headquarters of the Seventh Army in Le Mans and even with the headquarters of Army Group B in La Roche-Guyon. He argued that the 21st Panzer Division needed to be released, that our forces were being spread too thin, and that much valuable time was being lost. His face, though deep in concentration, twitched. There was only one thought on his mind: to go into action, to attack.

Eventually, the panzer division was placed under the command of the army corps and given the order to retake the coast. Lieutenant-General Feuchtinger initially carried out an attack from the east bank of the Orne, but he was unable to dislodge the enemy forces that had seized the Ranville–Bénouville bridge. This meant that he could not proceed with his plan of pivoting to the west and striking the British flank. He therefore crossed the river immediately to the north of Caen instead.

Marcks went to visit the panzer division at 1430 hours. Its preparatory measures were rather hesitant, with no fewer than five command cars having been reported as broken down. At 1700 hours, General Marcks met with a regimental commander and ordered that the attack was to go ahead. He personally led the 192nd Panzer Regiment from its assembly area. This was the only option after the breakdown of the command cars, for the effective employment of a panzer unit is dependent on the trouble-free transmission of orders and communications.

Our initial success was tremendous. The panzer troops penetrated the enemy front at 2000 hours and reached the coast at Luc. They established contact there with the strongpoints of the 716th Infantry Division, all of which had held on with grim determination in the midst of the hellish noise of bombs and naval artillery. Unfortunately, there were no reserves with which to maintain the momentum of our attack. The forces at our disposal were meagre. The British brought our attack to a halt, although their efforts were so costly that they had to send in roughly one hundred military gliders with additional troops and supplies directly into the attack sector. An utter state of confusion reigned. Everyone had to shoot and defend themselves in all directions, and we were soon in danger of running out of fuel and ammunition. The attack was broken off so that the panzer division, setting off for the south, would still have a chance of making it back through the rain of fire and re-establishing contact with the rear elements. This meant that the gains made against the British beachhead that day were lost. Also lost were about 25 per cent of the 150 armoured vehicles of the panzer division. The remaining vehicles reassembled to the north of Caen.

The advance carried out by the panzer division helped to reveal much about the enemy situation. Most of the prisoners taken belonged to the British 3rd Infantry Division and the Canadian 3rd Infantry Division, both of which were formations of the British I Corps. Our panzer thrust had separated these two divisions from one another. Other prisoners we had taken belonged to the British 4th Commando Brigade, the independent British 27th Armoured Brigade, and the armoured brigade of the British 79th Armoured Division. With the appearance of the first units of the British 50th (Northumbrian) Infantry Division and the British 7th Armoured Division on 7 June, it became clear that the forces landing near Caen were particularly strong. The third general staff officer of the LXXXIV Army Corps remarked: 'All that's needed now is the 1st Armoured Division and the 51st (Highland) Infantry Division, then Montgomery's old Eighth Army from North Africa will be here!' If these well-known units, which seemed to follow Field Marshal Rommel wherever he went, were to land on the coast of Calvados, there would be no question that we were in fact dealing with *the invasion*.

What was the situation in the air on 6 June? Nobody doubted that we would be numerically inferior in the air in the event of an invasion. This was apparent due to our inability to put a stop to enemy aircraft flying over northern France. Nevertheless, the degree of the superiority of the Allies in the air took us by surprise and caused us consternation. Never had we imagined that the enemy could launch thousands of sorties in one day or that the Luftwaffe would have only roughly 90 fighters and 70 bombers available in the West. Our army corps would receive no air support whatsoever in the American landing sector. The black-and-white cross had disappeared from the skies.

On 6 June, Allied fighter-bombers targeted anything that moved: small columns, food-carrier groups, vehicles, motorcycles, reconnaissance units, and messengers. Sometimes even ambulances, though they clearly displayed the red cross, were not spared. As the skies cleared towards the afternoon, the enemy conducted constant aerial reconnaissance over locations where he suspected our various headquarters were to be found. His objective was to bring about the paralysis of our operational leadership. So numerous were the enemy aerial sorties that the Luftwaffe signal centre in Caen abandoned any attempt to keep a record of them.

Since 1943, we had been aware of the remark made by Admiral Bertram Ramsay to the effect that the landing army would be a bullet fired by the navy. General Bernard Montgomery had added that naval superiority would be guaranteed once the battle in the air had been won. We also knew that the Allies had gained considerable experience in island-hopping in the Pacific. Even so, we could not help being overcome with fury over the fact that the enemy air forces could do as they pleased in our airspace. They enjoyed complete air supremacy.

The only active defence we had against enemy aircraft was in the form of the 25th Motorised Flak Regiment. It was equipped with the first-rate 8.8cm anti-aircraft gun, the best of its kind of weapon in the world and greatly feared by the enemy. While employed effectively, the men under the command of Colonel Ernst Hermann could not be everywhere at once. The batteries of the motorised flak regiment frequently had to change their positions, especially if there was cloud cover or if enemy aircraft started to fly beyond their firing range.

Our best method of passive defence was to make use of the apple orchards and hedgerows of Normandy. Thick canopies of leaves cast shadows and thereby concealed our forces. The many deeply cut dirt roads, overgrown with bushes, served as well-camouflaged trenches. It was with great accuracy that an enemy propaganda leaflet proclaimed that this landscape of orchards and meadows had never been so loved as by the Germans in 1944 and that, at the same time, the beautiful skies over that landscape had never been so cursed!

Feelings of melancholy prevailed when we recognised just how overwhelmingly decisive the impact of the enemy air forces would be. With relatively little risk, they bombed ground targets almost nonstop and hindered our ability to transmit communications by shooting the direction-finding stations of our observation outposts to pieces. They also inflicted heavy casualties on units that attempted to move by day. This meant that we could conduct movements only at night, while our supply traffic had to avoid main highways and was restricted to secondary roads. Fuel and ammunition were soon in short supply. Delays lasted for days rather than hours.

A report delivered personally to General Marcks by a master sergeant of the Luftwaffe at 0900 hours led to a significant error in the assessment of the situation and partly brought about unfavourable developments on the boundary between the 716th and 352nd Infantry Divisions. The master sergeant claimed that approximately 250 military gliders had touched down in the vicinity of his reconnaissance post in Lessay, and that he and his group had only just managed to escape. He was questioned thoroughly and stuck to his story.

Now it seemed as if airborne landings were taking place to the south-west on those meadows of Lessay, a region brushed by the salty sea wind and renowned for its lamb and mutton. We barely had any troops there! So dangerous was such a dramatic development that the report was passed on before the 30th Mobile Brigade in Coutances (under the command of Lieutenant-Colonel Hugo Freiherr von Aufseß), and the 752nd Infantry Regiment in Cérences (directly subordinate to the army corps) were to finish their reconnaissance missions. It became apparent a few hours later that the details of the report were wrong, but it would be a few more days before we fully understood what had happened. According to the statements provided by prisoners of war, the flight path of some of the military gliders from the Exeter–Newbury–Burford area took them past the northern side of the Channel Islands and over Lessay as they approached Sainte-Mère-Église from the west. In addition to this, numerous dummy paratroopers were subsequently dropped in the vicinity of Lessay. Although the army corps corrected the details of the situation in its evening report, General Marcks had already sent his reserve unit, the 915th Infantry Regiment, to deal with the non-existent threat. By the time the infantry regiment returned to resist the left wing of the British sector, it was too late.

A picture of the situation at the front was revealed in the early afternoon by the reports, or specifically the losses, of the coastal batteries that stood along the coast as far as the extensive cauliflower fields of Barfleur. The units in question were the 1254th, 1255th, and 1261st Army Coastal Artillery Battalions, as well as Naval Coastal Batteries Saint-Marcouf, Pernelle, and Longues. All had been subjected to air attack since the early morning. Their destruction would enable the Allied warships to sail closer to the coast and thus exploit fully their tremendous firepower in the support of the divisions that had landed.

While the defensive fight against the Americans progressed reasonably well, developments on the right wing of the army corps became far less favourable from 1500 hours. The evening situation report of the 716th Infantry Division highlighted why this was so. The bombardment at

0530 hours had significantly breached the defensive front, with large portions of our minefields having been set off and thereby rendered useless as obstacles. Smokescreens prevented our batteries from being able to open fire on the colossal vessels at sea. The result was that the British, though suffering heavy casualties, enjoyed far greater success in carrying out their seaborne landings than did the Americans. The enemy forces deliberately bypassed German strongpoints, wherever they still existed, on either side, cutting off their lines of communication and, sometimes days later, striking them from the rear.

The British would have some rather tough nuts to crack. The Luftwaffe strongpoint at Douvres was held by army units and Luftwaffe ground forces for a full 11 days, from 6 to 17 June. Every penetration of the front by the enemy threatened to develop into a full-scale breakthrough, for there existed no secondary German defensive line to the rear. On top of that, our lack of aerial reconnaissance and the counteraction of the RAF meant that our local reserves would be incapable of intervening effectively. Our defences had been severely weakened by the enemy aerial bombardment, with two panzer companies being annihilated at the outset. The initial successes achieved by the British were due neither to the element of surprise nor even to any failure on the part of the German 726th Infantry Regiment, but rather to the full exploitation by Montgomery of the tactical means at his disposal.

According to the appraisal of the situation by the Seventh Army, the point of main effort of the fighting lay to the west of the mouth of the Orne, between Caen and Ryes. In order to resolve the situation, the I SS Panzer Corps, commanded by SS-General Sepp Dietrich, was made available at 1600 hours. This formation comprised, alongside the 21st Panzer Division (Lieutenant-General Edgar Feuchtinger), the 12th SS Panzer Division Hitlerjugend (SS-Major-General Fritz Witt), which had just been moved forward from the area near Alençon and La Loupe, and the Panzer Lehr Division (Lieutenant-General Fritz Bayerlein). These forces were to be used to carry out a new counter-thrust after the one that had failed earlier in the day.

Any orders to be issued by the LXXXIV Army Corps would ideally contain the details of the situation, but such details were lacking. Because the information that came in was full of gaps, it was impossible to know precisely how events were unfolding at the front. In particular, the location of the point of main effort of the enemy armoured forces was not yet known. Those forces would be the trump card of the British defence the next day.

This agonising uncertainty prompted the third general staff officer of the army corps to set off and visit as many command posts as could still be reached. He wanted to see for himself what was happening so that he could complete or correct the situation map.

The headquarters drivers had adapted remarkably quickly to the circumstances created by enemy aerial operations, constantly exchanging their experiences with one another. As aerial surveillance subsided noticeably every day at 1430 hours, the drivers opined: 'They're now in England drinking their tea!' That was therefore the time the drivers would set off. The twisted and scorched metal frameworks of destroyed vehicles were frequently to be seen on the roadside. Most of them lay on their rear axles, resembling animals sitting on their hind legs. Burning tanks were also occasionally spotted, their paintwork boiling on hot steel. Ammunition wagons had lost their valuable cargo, and the carcasses of black-and-white or red cows were scattered around the lush green meadows. Unperturbed by all of this, signal troops moved in pairs across the terrain and repaired telephone lines that had been shot to pieces.

It was not long before enemy fighter-bombers swarmed in the skies like hornets once more. The gurgling sound of rockets being fired could be heard from afar, and bursts of fire flickered along the roads. The enemy machines zoomed out from the sun or shot like bullets from the horizon. Their speed was tremendous and had always been underestimated. It was often too late by the time their presence was noticed. The pilots constantly had their fingers on their triggers, ready to open fire with their 2cm cannons on anything that moved without cover. None of our fighters could catch them. One must have deep respect for the motorcycle messengers and orderly officers who defied the fighter-bombers from one day to the next!

The drive undertaken by the third general staff officer led along secondary roads that went around the battlefield and sometimes past groups of refugees heavily laden with white sheets. Crouching on their two-wheeled carts, the men gazed grimly at the skies, the women sobbed, and the children felt frightened. This picture of misery contrasted strongly with the common image of a prosperous Normandy.

Caen was under heavy fire, so the third general staff officer circled around it and Troarn and reached the Houlgate–Deauville–Trouville coastal road immediately to the east of Cabourg. It was there, with the 711th Infantry Division (Lieutenant-General Josef Reichert) in Pont-l'Évêque, that the sector of the LXXXI Army Corps, headquartered at Rouen, began. The drive ended at the outermost strongpoint, which lay in a picturesque setting near magnificent luxury villas on a pine-covered hill.

Although barely 3 kilometres from Army Field Gun Battery Merville, which had by then been captured by the enemy, it was surprisingly peaceful and idyllic. It was a spot that seemed to be isolated from the battle raging nearby. The flats at the mouth of the Orne appeared to be unoccupied. The only pieces of evidence of the fighting taking place were the dissipation of smoke in the misty and greyish blue air above distant villages, the barely audible fire of machine guns, and the dull and regular discharge of heavy naval guns.

The picture at sea was quite different. An observer at Riva-Bella would have been at a loss for words as he gazed through his binoculars at the landing sites. Riding at anchor in the water were large numbers of the Landing Ship Infantry (LSI). These were enormous transport vessels, and together they looked like one grey mass. A great deal of activity took place between those vessels and the coast. An uninterrupted stream of small special vehicles was to be seen. Troops, tanks, and supplies were constantly being lightered to shore. The smaller vehicles circled the larger vessels like chicks around hens, seemingly wavering somewhat in the mist. Minesweepers cleared large stretches of water of mines or, alternatively, carved paths through the minefields.

Off to the side, the silhouettes of anti-aircraft ships and gunboats could be discerned. They provided close artillery support to their forces, their guns flashing sharply every time they opened fire. Heavy gunfire, concealed somewhere in the mist, rumbled further to the west.

Our reports indicated that it came from the British battleship *Nelson* as well as from an old French warship that had been run aground on the sand. These ships covered the wings of the landing site and hurled their shells far inland. Many barrage balloons had been raised by the enemy in order to prevent the approach of low-flying German aircraft. Above them, Allied fighters dominated the skies. The level of activity was such that it was almost like the operations at a large harbour in peacetime.

There also lay many boats like dark stains on the beach. They had been shot to pieces or had become caught on, and were then capsized by, the foreshore obstacles as the tide ebbed.

Where was the Luftwaffe? Could there ever have been a better opportunity to strike and paralyse the amassed enemy forces? Was it not now the moment not only to relieve our comrades in the infantry and artillery who fought so hard, but also to cause the Allies to lose as much as possible as they attempted this invasion? The Allies had solved the problem of close cooperation between the three arms of the services. On top of that, they demonstrated astonishing efficiency in organisation.

The leadership of the US V Corps later summarised its assessment of the absence of German aircraft during the landings in Normandy:

> The complete absence of enemy air forces from the assault area was an outstanding feature of the D Day's action. It is easy to imagine what the intervention of enemy fighters and fighterbombers would have meant in the critical morning-hours, when the assault forces were crowed on the narrow beach flat. Allied air supremacy on D Day had been absolute.

On the return journey, a visit was paid to the command post of the 716th Infantry Division, and valuable details were provided by its third general staff officer, Major Wilhelm Wiegmann. After that it was on to Caen once more. This city would become the epitome of hell for the German and British troops who fought there. It lay in a plain amidst large grain fields and at a distance from the green landscapes that characterised western Normandy. Its beautiful old patrician houses with ornately carved wooden beams were engulfed by the shells that exploded and the firestorms that roared across the city. The destruction that was wrought defies description: 32cm projectiles caused multi-storey buildings to collapse like houses of cards. The district of Vaucelles in particular, with its bridges over the Orne and the nearby canal, was constantly subjected to the fire of heavy naval batteries.

It was into this inferno – through the swath of destruction, the flickering flames, and the smouldering houses – that the German infantry sprang into action. Above the smoke rose the towers of the sister churches Abbaye aux Hommes and Abbaye aux Dames, almost 900 years old, both of which were quintessential examples of Norman architecture. William the Conqueror is buried in the former. It was from there that he had invaded southern England in 1066.

The return trip ended just under a couple of hours later. As if to add insult to injury, the first evening report to arrive at the headquarters of the LXXXIV Army Corps was that of the 319th Infantry Division (Lieutenant-General Rudolf Graf von Schmettow), stationed on the Channel Islands, which stated simply: 'Nothing new.'

On top of all the concerns about the current situation, the question that occupied the minds at the headquarters of the army corps on the evening of 6 June 1944 was the same as that which was being asked at the headquarters of the Seventh Army and at that of Army Group B: was this really *the invasion* that was underway? Or was this merely a diversionary manoeuvre on a large scale, the objective of which was to compel us to commit our reserves prematurely and in the wrong place? Since the Allies enjoyed supremacy in the air and dominance at sea, they were able to determine the time and place not only of the main landing but also of any feint attack.

The High Command of the Wehrmacht (OKW) took the view that the main landing would take place in the Pas-de-Calais. There were good reasons to believe that this would indeed be the case, the most important of which was that the British and their Allies would arrive on the continent at the point closest to the Motherland. Their landing vehicles would be able to travel to and fro quickly and easily, while their fighters, with their short range, would have the best chance of being able to fly multiple sorties a day. Furthermore, with the Pas-de-Calais as the starting point for enemy ground forces, the Ruhr industrial area could be reached quickly and, as a result, German armaments production could be brought to a standstill earlier. However, there were also good reasons why the enemy might refrain from attempting a landing in the Pas-de-Calais, most significantly the tremendous strength of the German defensive installations opposite Dover as well as the presence of 19 divisions under the command of the Fifteenth Army.

The assumption that a second operation – the real invasion – was still in store prevailed until the middle of July. As a result, during the most decisive period, the Fifteenth Army simply remained on standby. Reserves were sent to Normandy in dribs and drabs in what amounted to tactical patchwork. Such an approach stood in stark contrast to the traditional brilliance of the general staff in operational thought and tactical performance. The decisions taken were strongly influenced by Hitler and went against sound military advice. It seemed that what had been hammered into every young lieutenant – do not take half measures! – had been forgotten. The OKW stuck to its preconceived opinion despite the fact that the best battle-tried troops of the Allies had been identified on the Cotentin Peninsula. The Americans possessed full-strength formations and the British the divisions of Montgomery. In addition, almost all enemy airborne units had gone into battle. The landing in Normandy could be nothing other than the main attack, which meant that the threat of any second landing would be nowhere near as great.

Friend and foe welcomed the light rain that fell on the evening of 6 June. Movement at the front came to a stop. Both sides were exhausted. German strongpoints behind the enemy lines held out, while some of the smaller groups fought their way through to the larger ones and thereby increased their defensive strength. Troops of the 919th Infantry Regiment withdrew across the bay outside Carentan, and the reports received from the formation provided a vivid image of what was unfolding. Nevertheless, the lack of certainty about the precise nature of the situation directly on the coast meant that only an estimate could be made as to how many strongpoints had fallen.

An arrangement was made with the neighbouring units – the LXXXI Army Corps of General of Panzer Troops Adolf-Friedrich Kuntzen in Rouen and the LXXIV Army Corps of General of Infantry Erich

Straube in Guingamp – neither of which had come under attack. All our concerns revolved around the question as to what would be faster: the growth in the number of enemy forces on the continent or the arrival of German reserves that had been made available? Such reserves would have to march at night whilst keeping away from the major highways. It was our hope, given that never in the history of warfare had there been an organisational and logistical challenge so great as that demanded by the Normandy landings, that the Allies would ultimately deplete their supplies.

The time had come for our quartermaster to do his utmost. Under cover of darkness, units shifted their positions, ammunition and fuel and rations were delivered, and prisoners and wounded were transported away. With the evacuation of the overcrowded field hospitals, the LXXXIV Army Corps assumed responsibility for many tasks that would have previously been looked after by the military administration headquarters in each of Cherbourg, Saint-Lô, and Caen.

It was from the hard Russian school of thought that our quartermaster had acquired considerable skill in mastering unforeseen situations. And there were indeed a number of difficulties he overcame every night: the assembly of new columns with almost the greatest of ease; the constant diversion of such columns in response to certain situations that arose (e.g. bombs falling on the original supply route, the front line edging too close to it, or bridges along it being destroyed); the allocation of frequently limited transport capacity; the extension of supply lines to intact railway stations; the prioritisation of deliveries to certain sectors of the front that were most in need; and the restriction of movements to the hours of the evening and the night.

Yet the enemy air forces did not sleep. By dropping photoflash bombs, they sought to take aerial photographs at night and thereby identify our movements. Flares were also dropped and remained in the air for several minutes, brilliantly illuminating our supply routes. The German troops christened them 'Christmas trees' due to their sparkling light. Important road junctions came under fire from long-range batteries. Nevertheless, compared to the day that had just passed, the night of 6/7 June was relatively relaxing.

The OKW issued the following communiqué in the Fatherland:

> The enemy commenced his attack against Western Europe overnight, something that he has been preparing and that we have been expecting for a long time. Initiated with heavy air strikes against our coastal fortifications, airborne landings were conducted in multiple locations along the northern coast of France between Le Havre and Cherbourg. Seaborne landings took place at the same time and with the support of strong naval forces. Fierce fighting is now underway in this sector of the coast.

CHAPTER 2

The battle of Cherbourg (7–26 June 1944)

As dawn broke on the second day, there had been little change in the situation in the American beachheads. Both sides continued to struggle for Sainte-Mère-Église. Unfortunately, when the Americans had lunged forward the day before, a flak unit had withdrawn from the combat zone and had therefore failed to defend the town. This gave an enemy parachute unit the opportunity to enter the town and set up a defensive position there. Our 91st Air Landing Division sent one of its battalions to carry out an attack, but it suffered heavy casualties at the hands of enemy aircraft and gained little ground as a result.

The struggle for Naval Coastal Battery Saint-Marcouf, equipped with three long-barrelled 21cm guns, was particularly fierce. This battery was one of the most important elements of our defence against an attack from the sea. In total, there were 33 battcries with 130 guns in the combat zone of the LXXXIV Army Corps. Sixteen of those batteries belonged to the army and the other 17 to the navy. Gun calibres varied considerably, with most of the army guns being between 10.5cm and 15.5cm and the navy guns 17cm and 30.5cm. The maximum firing range was 28 kilometres.

The enemy had long recognised the importance of the Saint-Marcouf battery. He had constantly taken aerial photographs of the site during its construction and had carried out an air raid against it with approximately one hundred heavy bombers several weeks before the commencement of the invasion. The sight of the surrounding landscape filled with what looked like lunar craters gave us a foretaste of what was to come.

Thankfully, the gun crews, under the command of naval lieutenant Walter Ohmsen, had sheltered in their bunkers in time and had suffered no losses. On 6 June, shortly after midnight, a company of the US 502nd Parachute Infantry Regiment landed in the vicinity of the village of Saint-Marcouf. At 0130 hours, a small reconnaissance patrol of our naval troops took the company leadership prisoner, while the remaining hundred or so paratroopers were hurled out of the village by the orderly officer and eight men of the II Battalion of the 919th Infantry Regiment. This ensured the safety of the battery, which at 0712 hours succeeded in sinking an enemy cruiser. The destroyers that sought to help came under the well-aimed fire of the 4th Battery of Army Coastal Artillery Regiment Triepel, so they veered away and laid down a smokescreen. In the meantime, the Saint-Marcouf battery prevented the enemy from being able to provide any further naval support to the troops that had landed, thereby playing an important role in bringing about the crisis for the Americans at Utah Beach. Even so, by the evening, its three long-barrelled guns had been put out of action. The battery itself held out for another five days thanks to the support of elements of the 6th Company of the 919th Infantry Regiment and managed to repel two major ground attacks launched by the enemy. After the second attack, with 90 of their men taken prisoner by the garrison, the Americans fell back to Dodainville. On 11 June, in accordance with the orders issued by the 709th Infantry Division, the naval artillerymen withdrew alongside the army infantrymen to the main line of resistance that lay to the north. The abandoned fortification fell into the hands of the enemy shortly thereafter.

Further to the south, the US 4th Infantry Division strove to fight its way through to the pockets held by American paratroopers. This division was an elite unit of the US Army, the traditions of its regiments reaching back to 1798, 1838, and 1866. Nevertheless, it made little headway, its main success being the seizure of Turqueville. Located there like a thorn in the side of the enemy was the strongpoint of the 795th Georgian Battalion. The Georgians put up tough resistance to begin with, so the Americans decided to achieve with words what they could not with weapons! A negotiator with a good command of the Georgian language persuaded the garrison to give up the fight, which enabled the US 4th Infantry Division to establish contact with some of the paratroopers. Leaflets that were later dropped on our lines made it clear that one of the Georgians, a former Russian general staff officer, had, with the aid of a map, provided details to the Americans regarding the surroundings.

The rapid fall of the Georgian strongpoint prevented the assault battalion of the Seventh Army from being able to break through to Turqueville. This meant that the assault battalion, which was under the command of Major Hugo Messerschmidt and subordinate to the 709th Infantry Division, was denied the opportunity of shattering the enemy parachute units.

The crisis that had developed for the Americans the day before on the coast of Calvados continued to affect them. The enemy troops in the vicinity of the village of Vierville were subjected to heavy artillery fire and were unable to move any further. Only along the heavily bombed terrain right next to the beach could those troops establish contact with the Americans who had entered the nearby Pointe du Hoc. It would not be until the following day that enemy armoured spearheads crossed the N13 highway and pressed forward to the northern side of the overflowing valley of the Aure, which had originally been the objective to be reached in the first 24 hours. This sector of the front caused the LXXXIV Army Corps the least concern, and it was our hope that we might even be able to erase the enemy forces there from our maps.

Further to the east, the US 1st Infantry Division reached an 8-kilometre stretch, between Tour-en-Bessin and Formigny, of the Caen–Carentan country road, but it failed for the time being to establish contact with the British. The German forces sitting between the Americans and the British consisted of elements of the 915th Infantry Regiment (of the 352nd Infantry Division), the 30th Mobile Brigade, and the I Battalion of the 726th Infantry Regiment, and they held Port-en-Bessin as well as the high ground on either side of the Drôme, which flowed from south to north. This German finger-like position represented a constant threat to the American and British flanks. For this reason, the Allies attacked on either side of the base of the finger on the afternoon of 8 June with the idea of cutting it off. Late in the evening, the German forces there

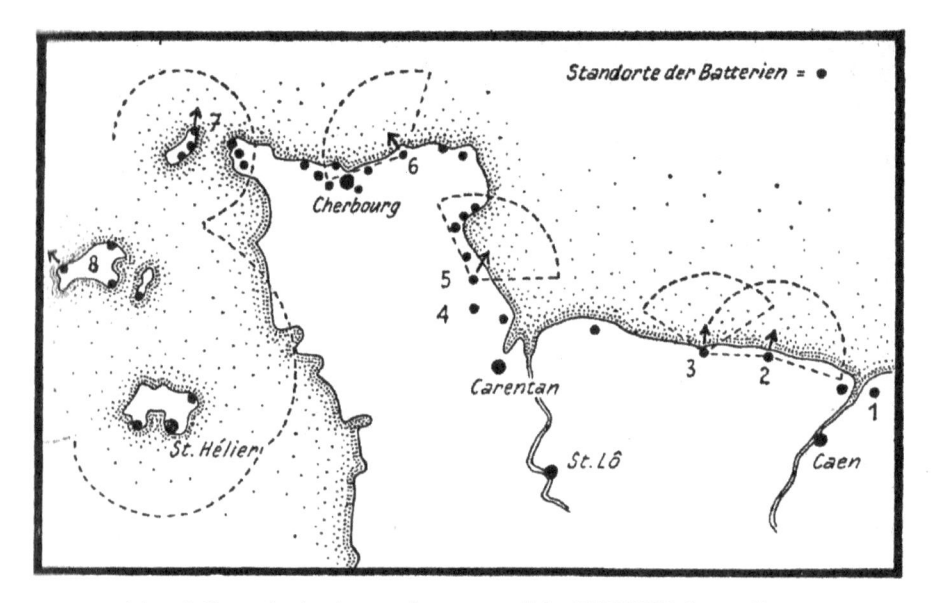

Map 4: Batteries in the combat zone of the LXXXIV Army Corps

1. Army Field Gun Battery Merville   4–7.5 cm
2. Army Coastal Battery Graye   4–12.2 cm
3. Naval Coastal Battery Longues   4–15.2 cm
4. Army Coastal Battery Azeville   4–10.5 cm
5. Naval Coastal Battery Saint-Marcouf 3–21 cm
6. Naval Coastal Battery Hamburg   4–24 cm
7. Naval Coastal Battery Elsaß   3–17 cm
8. Naval Coastal Battery Mirus   4–30.5 cm

received the order to evacuate the position. An American unit, which according to the statements provided by prisoners of war was L Company of the US 26th Infantry Regiment, sought to hinder the withdrawal of the German forces, but it was overrun and neutralised. By 0300 hours on 9 June, the position had been evacuated and the Americans and the British had established contact with one another.

Bayeux fell at noon on 8 June. A signals communications female auxiliary at the telephone exchange in the city immediately reported to the headquarters of the army corps the arrival of the British 50th (Northumbrian) Infantry Division. She held the mouthpiece out of the window and said: 'Major, do you hear the engine noises? The British tanks are driving by below us. I have to go now.' The third general staff officer agreed: 'I think that's a good idea. How will you get out?' She replied: 'Oh, I'll go through the back garden.'

More dangerous was the development of the situation in the vicinity of Caen. Early on 7 June, the 21st Panzer Division carried out the second panzer counter-thrust in conjunction with the few elements of the 12th SS Panzer Division Hitlerjugend that had arrived. That there was neither time to prepare properly nor support from the air had to be put up with, and it was not long before the counter-attack was brought to a halt by enemy artillery fire. The Panzer Lehr Division rolled forward on 8 June. This unit was commanded by Lieutenant-General Fritz Bayerlein, formerly Rommel's chief of staff in North Africa. Although it had departed the area near Le Mans on the evening of 6 June and had proceeded northwards over the Vire, only by the morning of 8 June did its leading elements reach a position immediately to the east of Tilly. This was a day later than originally planned, for the unfavourable situation in the air made progress slow. When it eventually carried out its attack, the Panzer Lehr Division lunged far forward into the boundary position between the Americans and the British, but it was soon compelled to withdraw to the area east of Tilly-sur-Seulles due to the complete exposure of its deep right flank.

It was the lack of time available to organise and carry out a united counter-attack that led to the isolated and hastily executed panzer thrusts of 6, 7, and 8 June. The enemy had established and expanded his

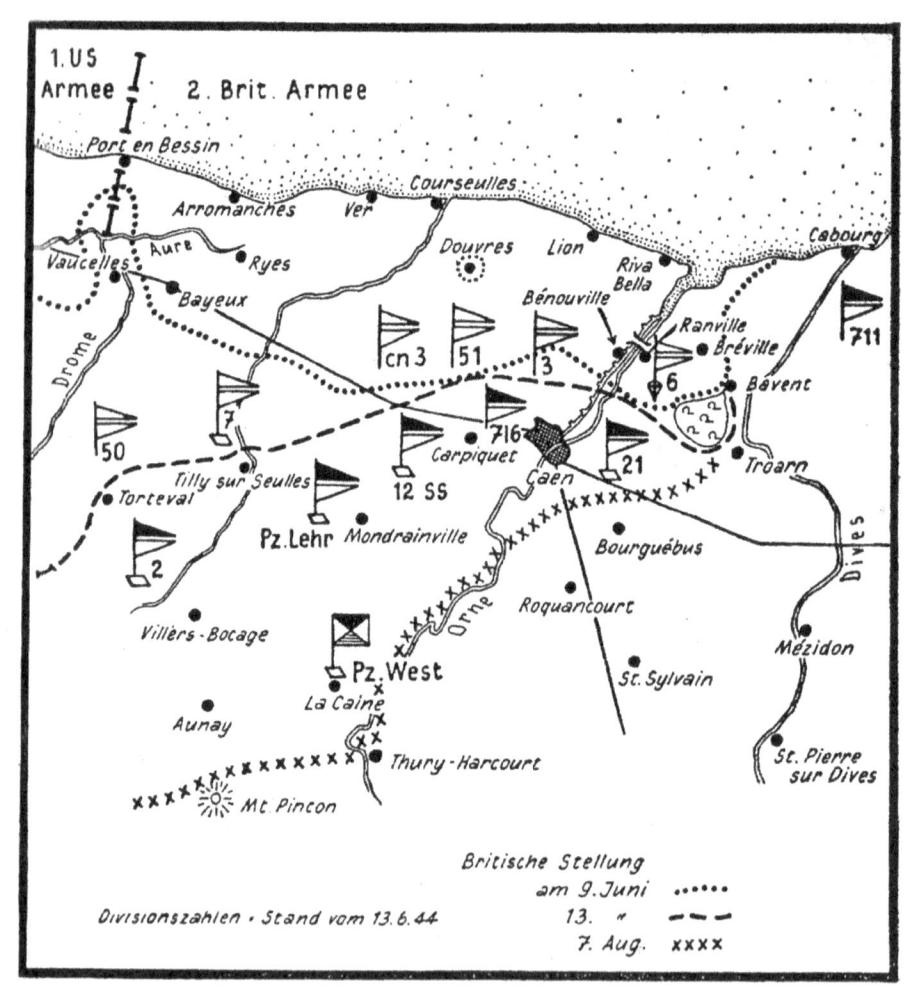

Map 5: The area around Caen

beachheads on the coast of Calvados with relative ease on those critical days. The statements provided by the prisoners we had taken consistently revealed how worried the enemy had been about the possibility of powerful German counter-measures, and this was why he had put considerable effort into dominating the skies. He thereby succeeded in slowing the approach of our reserves and in dampening the strength of any counter-strike we might attempt. The most we could do was intercept the attacker and bring his advance to a standstill.

On 8 June, Army Group B ordered that the zone of command be split. The right wing of the British sector and the entire American sector would remain the responsibility of the LXXXIV Army Corps, which was given the support of the II Parachute Corps (General of Parachute Troops Eugen Meindl) a few days later. The front to the east of the Dives and extending as far as Tilly was taken over by Panzer Group West (General of Panzer Troops Leo Freiherr Geyr von Schweppenburg). The headquarters of the panzer group in La Caine, which lay 6 kilometres north-east of Thury-Harcourt, was spotted by the enemy as early as 9 June and destroyed in an air raid on 10 June. Only General von Schweppenburg, though wounded, escaped with his life. His chief of staff and 17 staff officers were killed. It was not until the end of June that the newly reorganised headquarters of the panzer group was ready to take charge of the sector of the front that extended from the Orne to almost as far as the Vire. This sector roughly corresponded with the British one.

In the interim, in order to deal with the unclear state of the chain of command that had been brought about, the German Army Command in the West (OB West), in agreement with Army Group B, recommended to the OKW a reorganisation of forces and areas of responsibility. As recorded in the war diary of OB West on 12 June 1944:

> An army detachment would be created from the headquarters of the LXXXIV Army Corps and would be assigned responsibility for the entire combat zone and for all the troops and units committed there. Since General of Artillery Marcks was killed while on his way to visit the front, OB West would be unable to implement its plan of putting him in charge of this combat zone.

The commander of Army Group B, Field Marshal Erwin Rommel, decided that our defensive efforts would be concentrated in the vicinity of Caen, for it was there that we anticipated the main enemy attack. He saw to it that panzer divisions, army artillery units (including railway guns), two rocket launcher brigades, and one flak corps were committed to the area. This ensured that our defence possessed some degree of depth.

Meanwhile, additional infantry divisions started to arrive in the combat zone of the LXXXIV Army Corps. One of them was the 77th Infantry Division under Lieutenant-General Rudolf Stegmann, a formation with which the leadership of the army corps was familiar. General Marcks had overseen its creation in February 1944, and it was trained specifically for combat in the hedgerow terrain. It had been transferred to the LXXIV Army Corps on 1 May so that it could strengthen the defence of the stretch of coast in Brittany between Avranches and Saint-Brieuc. Only a few battalions of eastern troops had been stationed there before then.

The 77th Infantry Division immediately set off on the morning of the day of the invasion for the heathland in the vicinity of Lessay. Enemy aerial activity meant that the elements of the infantry division ended up being spread out across 200 kilometres! Although the leading elements reached Valognes on 9 June, the bulk of the divisional forces remained as far back as Avranches. Only on the fifth day could all the regiments assemble, and they established themselves along the upper course of the Merderet with an eastward-facing front. One air strike after another had already caused the loss of most of the vehicles of the infantry division while it had been making its way northwards. Since transportation by rail so close to the combat zone had not been an option, the exhausted troops had been compelled to march at night.

The situation was similar for other units that were transferred from Brittany to the front, namely the 3rd Parachute Division (from Carhaix), the 265th Infantry Division (from the area near Lorient and Vannes), and Battle Group Heinz of the 275th Infantry Division (from the area near Saint-Nazaire and Redon). The latter battle group consisted of a regiment reinforced with two batteries and two pioneer battalions. Both infantry divisions had to detrain after having barely covered a quarter of the distance of their journey. It was due to the belief of the OKW that a larger landing was still to be conducted by the enemy in the Pas-de-Calais that the reinforcements sent to Normandy were drawn from the most distant part of Brittany. Not one of the many divisions under the command of the Fifteenth Army was made available.

The LXXXIV Army Corps waited for days and in vain for the arrival of the 17th SS Panzer Grenadier Division Götz von Berlichingen (commanded by SS-Lieutenant-General Werner Ostendorff). This SS division was headed towards the Isigny–Carentan area with the objective of preventing the Americans from crossing the mouth of the canalised Vire and thus from uniting their two beachheads to the south of the bay outside Carentan into a larger whole. The SS panzer grenadier troops had departed their assembly area in Thouars, which lay to the south of Saumur (on the Loire), as early as 7 June, and they experienced many problems while on their way to the front. The already insufficient number of vehicles at their disposal was reduced considerably. On 10 June, the advance detachments of the SS division were stuck in Saint-Lô because of a shortage of fuel, which meant that they were unable to exploit the diminished effectiveness of enemy aircraft in the misty weather that prevailed at that moment.

On the defensive front in the vicinity of Montebourg, the US VII Corps felt its way forward towards the north. In the account that follows of the fighting that took place, three locations stand out: Azeville, Montebourg, and Quinéville.

Stationed in Azeville was a strongpoint of Army Coastal Artillery Regiment Triepel. The battery there, under the command of Lieutenant Hans Kattnig and armed with 10.5cm guns, managed to hold on to its position for four days. The blockhouses were skilfully camouflaged with ordinary stonework. Thanks to the fact that the cables leading to the strongpoint had survived the carpet bombing, it was possible for the Azeville battery, the surrounding batteries, and the 100th Nebelwerfer Regiment to properly coordinate their fire. On 7 June, a determined attack conducted by the US 12th Infantry Regiment (of the US 4th Infantry Division) resulted in failure and heavy losses, with approximately 300 killed in action. Little by little, heavy naval artillery shot the blockhouses to pieces. Then, on 9 June, the enemy suddenly concentrated his artillery fire, with approximately 1,500 shells raining down on the strongpoint. This was followed by a final attack supported by flame-throwing units. The German forces at the strongpoint swiftly surrendered, for they had by that time expended their ammunition.

In the vicinity of Montebourg, elements of the 709th Infantry Division, the 91st Air Landing Division, and the 77th Infantry Division were positioned to the south of the Sinope. The town itself was held only by the headquarters company of the 919th Infantry Regiment, but the Americans approached it hesitantly. They had been deceived by a clever manoeuvre arranged by the commander of the 709th Infantry Division, Lieutenant-General Karl-Wilhelm von Schlieben, who had 20 old French tracked vehicles drive in and around the town during the night so as to produce tank noises that could be heard far and wide. This convinced the enemy to come to a halt the next day despite the overwhelming strength of the pressure he could have applied. Although the men of the headquarters company had grown unaccustomed to war prior to the enemy invasion, they now surpassed themselves. The captain in charge of the company blinked in amazement when two of his men, armed only with carbines and blocking one of the entrances to the town, succeeded in putting an American armoured reconnaissance car, occupied by a lieutenant and three men, out of action.

On 13 June, Army Group B reported:

> For days, there has been nonstop heavy fire from naval artillery off the east coast of the Cotentin Peninsula against the flank and rear of our forces holding the Montebourg–Quinéville line. Air strikes against those forces have also been constant. Even the best troops cannot continue to bear a burden like this if they have suffered such heavy losses and have no counter-measures at their disposal.

Our defensive cornerstone on the coast, Quinéville, fell on 14 June. The commencement of the enemy thrust towards the harbour of Cherbourg loomed on the horizon. In the area to the west of the Merderet, along the line connecting Le Ham and Pont l'Abbé, there already stood three American formations: the 90th Infantry Division, the 9th Infantry Division, and the 82nd Airborne Division. It was clear that they were preparing to lunge to the west.

In the central sector of the LXXXIV Army Corps, the pressure applied by the enemy in the direction of Saint-Lô was growing in intensity. He captured Isigny on 9 June. American tanks drove through the ever-weaker lines of the 352nd Infantry Division (Lieutenant-General Dietrich Kraiß) and arrived at the railway station in Lison, which lay on the main line between Cherbourg and Caen. A handful of tanks pushed a little further until their crews became suspicious of how quiet it was, so they held their positions along the Elle at a point just 10 kilometres to the north of Saint-Lô. They could have easily rolled straight on to the headquarters of the army corps, for the only reserves available to us at that moment were the troops of the headquarters company. There were rumours going around to the effect that the noise of enemy tracked vehicles could be clearly heard only 1.5 kilometres away from the command post of the army corps. Measures were taken to quickly secure the southern end of the destroyed bridge that had led over the stretch of the Vire that flowed through the city. After that, we started to pack in preparation for the first relocation of the headquarters of the army corps, and this took place at 1400 hours in broad daylight and with the sun shining brilliantly. The new headquarters was set up in a tunnel, completely damp and still under construction, below the seminary in Agneaux, which lay on the west bank of the Vire. This stalactite-filled cavern, the lighting in which failed all the time, would remain the heart of the leadership of the army corps for more than a week.

A welcome visitor came the next day. The third general staff officer of OB West, Lieutenant-Colonel Wilhelm Meyer-Detring, wanted to obtain for himself a picture of the situation, and we were able to present to him a captured copy of an American document outlining the enemy assessment of our ground forces. He grinned when he saw how the enemy had been deceived by our use of dummy divisions, and he also noted with interest how the history of each of our divisions was described. There was full recognition in this document of the excellent performance of the German Army in Russia.

However, the most important document had already been captured on 8 June. A landing boat that had been shot to pieces washed ashore in the combat zone of the 439th Eastern Battalion in the vicinity of

Géfosse-Fontenay. In it were the corpses of several American naval officers, including that of a beachmaster, an officer responsible for the disembarkation of troops and munitions in amphibious warfare. Amongst his gear was a stack of papers that was immediately sent to the army corps for evaluation. The third general staff officer of the army corps could hardly believe his ears when both interpreters approached him a short time later and called out: 'We have the operational plan of the US VII Corps!' That was indeed the case: the entire plan was there for us to look at. Every single phase from D-Day onwards was laid out in detail, with objectives to be reached and dates for those objectives. Even though this plan dealt primarily with the Cotentin Peninsula, its discovery was a stroke of luck of the kind that rarely happens.

Beyond the details of the planned employment of the US VII Corps, the German leadership was able to gain an insight into the intentions of the enemy in general. He would aim to secure the area between the coast and the series of dams along the Groult, Douve, and Merderet Rivers, after which he would try to thrust to the west coast and pivot to the north in order to take the harbour of Cherbourg from the rear. It was clear from the document that the US VII Corps and V Corps would seek to unite their beachheads and thereby create a continuous landing sector through Bayeux that would join up with the combat zone of the British XXX Corps. The captured document was immediately duplicated for distribution to the subordinate divisions, and the first general staff officer of the army corps personally delivered a copy to the headquarters of the Seventh Army.

Under ordinary combat conditions, such a discovery would have been extremely valuable. The enemy remained unaware of the loss of the document and therefore adhered to his original plan. He reached his objectives much more slowly than intended, and that continued to be the case even when the number of divisions he had in the field had doubled. Nevertheless, our numerical inferiority in men and materiel, combined with the complete absence of the Luftwaffe, meant that there was little that we could do other than gnash our teeth as the realisation of the enemy operational plan took place step by step.

The N13 highway ran along the coast through Carentan and would therefore be of no use to the enemy for as long as we maintained our hold on the town. The objective most urgently to be pursued by the Americans would no doubt be to unite their two landing zones, thereby eliminating any threat we could pose to their inner flanks. The US 502nd Parachute Infantry Regiment, which belonged to the US 101st Airborne Division, arduously fought its way southwards from Saint-Côme-du-Mont along the highway, going through the lowland area and over the dam. Enemy aircraft, in conjunction with air-directed artillery fire, suppressed the small number of German strongpoints on either side of the highway, and it was up to the enemy troops to push across four bridges (one over the Douve, another over the Madeleine, and the remaining two over runoff channels). Each day, those troops repeated the same process, blasting gaps in our front during the day and making small leaps forward at dusk. Gradually, the enemy established a position to the south of the lowland area. Both sides suffered heavy casualties. The wind carried the cries of wounded Americans.

Resisting this enemy advance was the 6th Parachute Regiment (Major Friedrich August Freiherr von der Heydte), a formation that had fought at Monte Cassino. The combat conditions in Normandy were far worse than they had been in central Italy. It had been possible in the latter to find cover in good shelters or rocky grottos, and the protection provided by German anti-aircraft guns had been effective in keeping enemy fighter-bombers at high altitudes and thereby preventing them from being able to hit targets with pinpoint accuracy. In Normandy, however, the paratroopers were exposed in open terrain. Enemy aircraft dominated the skies, and it was not easy to dig in anywhere. The only real defensive line was formed by the outskirts of Carentan, although it could be observed without difficulty by enemy artillery. The forwardmost obstacle of the parachute regiment was in a large orchard on a farm immediately to the south-west of the first bridge. This position was held for several days, and only on the afternoon of 11 June did the defenders fall back in response to the pressure applied by the enemy. The lively fire of our rear-guard units concealed our withdrawal from the Americans and made them approach the outskirts of the town with the utmost caution. Earmarked for the provision of support to the 6th Parachute Regiment was a battle group of the 17th SS Panzer Grenadier Division Götz von Berlichingen, which at that moment already stood to the north of Périers.

The evacuation of Carentan came as rather a shock to the headquarters of the army corps. It was only the day before that the parachute regiment had been commended in the Wehrmacht communiqué. This formation had been given clear orders to hold on to the town at all costs until the arrival of the SS battle group, but now it had suddenly abandoned its key position! General Marcks was at that time visiting another sector of the front, so the chief of staff of the army corps immediately made his way to the headquarters of the parachute regiment to discuss the possibility of carrying out a counter-attack. The reason given for the withdrawal was that our artillery was in danger of running out of ammunition. Although there was sufficient additional ammunition stored in the surrounding woods, it could not be brought to the battery positions at the front quickly enough.

In the meantime, General Marcks waited impatiently for the return of his chief of staff. When the chief of staff finally did so, the general had the following to say:

> I fully agree with the measures you have taken, but, until further notice, please do not leave the command post again if you are the only one here. It is necessary to keep someone alive who has a thorough understanding of the overall situation in Normandy. What has taken place in Carentan is quite disturbing. Despite achieving little territorial gain, the enemy has managed to establish a firm connection between his two beachheads. Tomorrow is the sixth day of the invasion. If nothing on the battlefield can be decided in our favour before then, there will be little our army corps can do to prevent fate taking its course. I would then recommend to the Seventh Army that the forces of the army corps move northwards into the peninsula so that the supply harbour in Cherbourg can be held. This would leave the south open, but we cannot be everywhere at once. I will drive to the Carentan front tomorrow morning in order to oversee preparations for the recapture of the town.

During the night, the Americans carried out a large-scale concentric attack whose spearheads thrust forward on either side of Carentan and met up at 0730 hours at Hill 30, which lay in La Billonnerie and on the road to Périers. Standing there was an eastern battalion, but it soon fled. Its German commander had fallen in battle.

At 0930 hours on 12 June, the car that would take General Marcks to the front stopped outside the tunnel. The chief of staff spoke to him before he left: 'I respectfully request the general not to expose himself to too much danger. A change in our leadership would be disastrous.' The general replied: 'You and your life! We can die respectfully as soldiers on the battlefield, but our poor Fatherland!' With that he left.

Barely had the driver turned off from the avenue in the seminary and onto the road than the rumble of rockets fired by a Typhoon and the bursts of machine-gun fire of several more fighter-bombers could be heard. A short time later, the bitter news of what had happened was brought to us by one of the passengers of the vehicle, an officer in charge of general staff training. Although the sun was shining, there had been ground mist at first, and the general had ordered that the main road be used instead of secondary roads so that the front could be reached more quickly. The mist suddenly cleared while they were driving alongside a stream 3 kilometres to the west of Saint-Lô. Enemy aircraft that had been circling above hit the car shortly before it could reach the cover of the hedges that lay ahead. A 2cm projectile tore through the arteries in the general's right leg near his groin. There was nothing that could be done to save him, and he bled to death in the roadside ditch towards 0945 hours. It was thus that one of the finest minds in the German military passed away. After almost one week of fierce fighting, the army corps had lost its revered commander.

The staff of the army corps bid farewell to their commander at midnight. In the distance, roughly in the vicinity of the mouth of the Vire, smoke and flames were to be seen, while to be heard was the broken drone of enemy aircraft as they followed their flight paths across the night sky. Muffled battery fire was interrupted by the sharp cracks of our volleys as the plain coffin was borne by the non-commissioned officers of our headquarters and lowered into the grave at the foot of the statue of the Virgin Mary in the garden of the seminary. The closest colleagues of General Marcks were in attendance, and a few words of the Austrian dramatist Franz Grillparzer came to mind for the third general staff officer that the general had once quoted to him in a moment of reflection: 'This is how man meets his end, and the only thing we can take with us from the struggle of life is the insight into nothing!'

The loss of its commander was not the only misfortune for the army corps on 12 June. On its right wing, the US V Corps had advanced as far as the entire length of the valley of the Aire and had reached the multiple road junction in Litteau, which lay near the south-western edge of Forêt de Cerisy. It was becoming clear that the enemy was seeking to envelop our key position in Saint-Lô from the east, in the combat zone of our 3rd Parachute Division. The ultimate objective of the Americans would be to establish a wide, secure, and unified front with the British, who themselves were engaged in heavy fighting in the Tilly–Caumont–Balleroy area. The British 7th Armoured Division rushed forward to Villers-Bocage, but its deep flank was struck just in time by our 2nd Panzer Division (Lieutenant-General Heinrich Freiherr von Lüttwitz). The enemy troops were chased back to Torteval, 8 kilometres to the north of Villers-Bocage. It would be several days before a revival of the fighting on this sector of the front took place.

The new commander of the LXXXIV Army Corps, General of Artillery Wilhelm Fahrmbacher, arrived on the evening of 12 June. He had until then been the commander of the XXV Army Corps, whose forces held Brittany and whose headquarters was in Pontivy. His first measure was the execution of the counter-attack on Carentan. Although postponed until the following day so that the heavy weaponry of the 17th SS Panzer Grenadier Division Götz von Berlichingen could be brought forward and utilised, the counter-attack failed. The support that had been promised by the Luftwaffe failed to materialise, and the replacements at our disposal were inexperienced and unable to cope with the difficult task they had been assigned. As a result, the situation on the Cotentin Peninsula had become ever more critical.

We will now turn our attention to the events in the vicinity of Cherbourg. In order to hold on to the city and prevent the supply harbour there from falling into the hands of the Allies, a directive that had been issued by the Führer and had been repeated on 9 June stipulated that four divisions were to put up as much resistance as possible and then conduct a fighting withdrawal to the north with the objective of defending the harbour installations. It was not a hasty retreat that would be carried out; instead, delaying action would be employed and ground would be yielded gradually. The four divisions that had been given this task were the 709th Infantry Division, the 243rd Infantry Division, the 77th Infantry Division, and the 91st Air Landing Division. Since the Americans were now in possession of Carentan and were pushing westwards from their bridgehead in the direction of La Haye-du-Puits, there existed the very real danger that the forces of the LXXXIV Army Corps would be split in two.

General Fahrmbacher and his chief of staff struggled over the question as to whether the army corps should move to the north and defend Cherbourg from a line far in front of the harbour or whether it should seal off the peninsula at its narrowest point further south and leave only a smaller force in its northern part. To do both would have been beyond the ability of the army corps. In view of the predominantly horse-drawn units at its disposal, the army corps recommended to the Seventh Army that the separation of forces ought not to be forced by the enemy but rather carried out on our own initiative. The Seventh Army and Army Group B completely agreed with this recommendation, but it was repeatedly rejected by the OKW even though our forces would end up being divided one way or another.

The eventual result was a great success for the enemy. His right wing, composed of multiple tank brigades and supported by aircraft and artillery, overran the German security positions at Saint-Sauveur-le-Vicomte, and it was on 18 June that forces belonging to the US 9th Infantry Division and US 3rd Armored Division reached the west coast of the peninsula in the vicinity of Barneville and Carteret. With that, the forces of the LXXXIV Army Corps, including those of the first-rate 77th Infantry Division, were cut in two. An American corridor had come into being, forming a northern and southern interdiction front that isolated Cherbourg.

The disagreement that had arisen due to the different tactical views within the German leadership led to a real tug-of-war. Orders and countermands repeatedly went to and fro. The frequent failure of telephone lines exacerbated the situation, as did the jamming or overlapping of radio communications. The command posts of our units, often on the move, lacked mobile radio equipment. Orderly officers, and even the chief of staff of the army corps, exerted a great deal of energy into ensuring the successful transmission of orders. They ventured forward at night to deliver orders to divisional command posts even when their locations were not precisely known. It was often the case that units had already started to move regardless of any orders they might have previously received. The constant back and forth of orders not only weakened our units through unnecessary movements, but also eroded the confidence of our field commanders in the ability of the supreme command.

On 16 June, southern England and the city of London were bombarded for the first time with a new type of heavy explosive device: the V-1 flying bomb. A number of these had been launched by the 155th Flak Regiment, commanded by Colonel Max Wachtel, and it was greatly hoped by the headquarters of the army corps that this weapon would bring about a change in our fortunes.

At 1000 hours, Rommel arrived at the command post of the army corps. Once General Fahrmbacher and his chief of staff had provided an update on the situation, the field marshal said: 'I give my approval for the separation of the groups. To try to hold on to everything here would mean to lose everything!' However, during the time he was still at the headquarters of the army corps, Rommel received a telephone call that informed him of a strict order reissued by the OKW to the effect that the current lines were to be held. 'Even I am powerless against a Führer directive!' he said.

A reorganisation of forces was necessary to accommodate what was happening on the battlefield. In the vicinity of Quinéville, Valognes, and Le Ham were the 709th Infantry Division and the 922nd Grenadier Regiment (of the 243rd Infantry Division), so these were united into a Battle Group Cherbourg and placed under the command of Lieutenant-General von Schlieben. In order to avoid any confusion, OB West made it clear that responsibility for the northern part of the Cotentin Peninsula and thus for Cherbourg lay solely with the commander of Battle Group Cherbourg.

The 77th Infantry Division and the 91st Air Landing Division were brought together as Battle Group Hellmich and were to be led by the former commander of the 243rd Infantry Division, Lieutenant-General Heinz Hellmich. The task of the battle group would be to prevent a breakthrough by the Americans to the south. We wanted to transfer a reinforced battle group of the 319th Infantry Division from the Channel Islands to the continent, but our proposals along these lines were rejected due to Hitler's insistence that the Channel Islands were not to be weakened under any circumstances. Battle Group Hellmich would therefore have to carry out the task it had been given on its own, so it commenced preparatory measures. It evacuated areas being seized by the Americans and conducted reconnaissance in the hills of the Prairies Marécageuses so as to determine the best positions for our artillery units and command posts. By the time our forces acted independently, voluntarily splitting into two in the manner that had been foreseen by the army corps, it was thanks to these preparatory measures that a new line of resistance could be established quickly.

The US 82nd Airborne Division established a bridgehead across the Douve at Saint-Sauveur-le-Vicomte on 16 June. Its flank ran alongside and was therefore protected by the swampy terrain of the Prairies Marécageuses. Any counter-thrusts attempted by German forces from the south were stopped by the US Eighth Air Force, and it was during an enemy air attack on 17 June that Lieutenant-General Hellmich was killed. A projectile fired by a fighter-bomber had split his skullcap. This made him the third general in the army corps who had fallen since the commencement of the Normandy landings.

It was not long before the enemy had gained ground behind the right flank of the 77th Infantry Division. The army corps therefore ordered the infantry division to disengage and withdraw to the area south of the Portbail–Doville line. Should this not be possible, the infantry division was to fall back towards Cherbourg. The divisional commander, Lieutenant-General Rudolf Stegmann, got in touch with the fortress commandant, but his liaison officer reported that the circumstances in the harbour had not made a good impression on him. In any case, the infantry division probably would have hindered rather than helped the

52 • NORMANDY

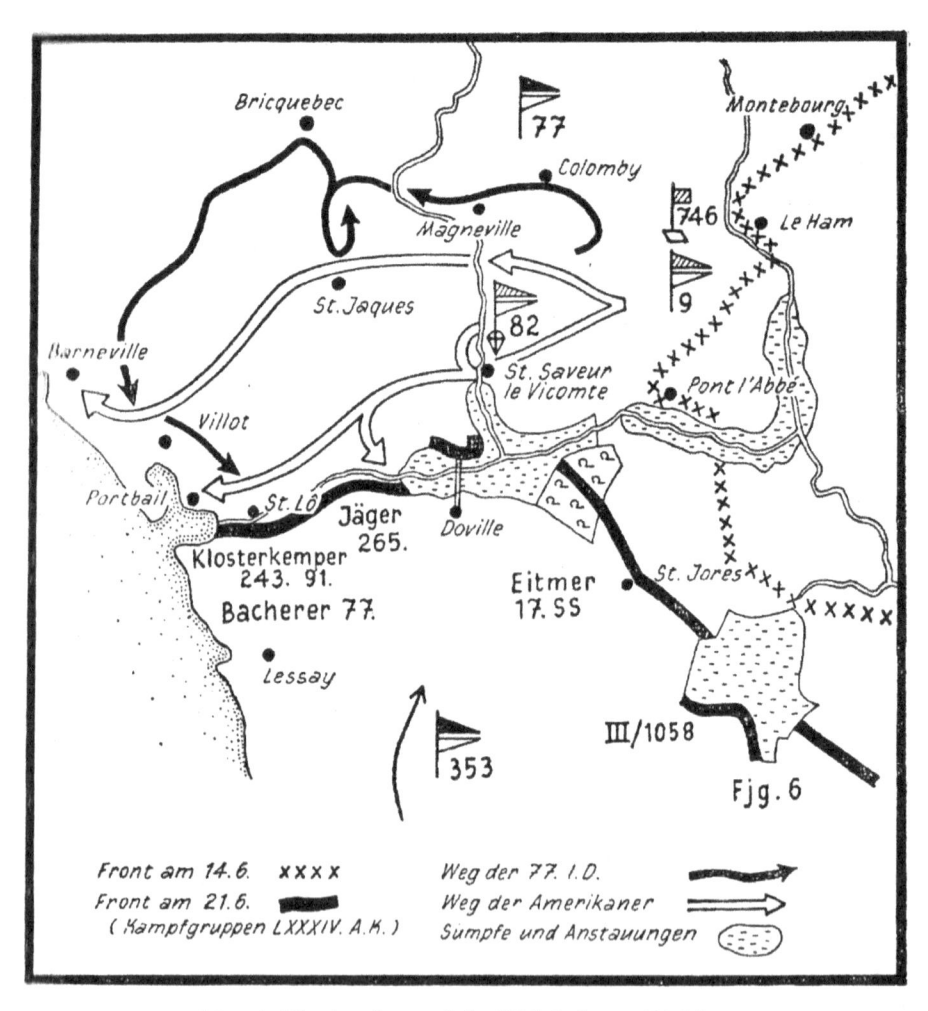

Map 6: The breakout of the 77th Infantry Division

effort to hold Fortress Cherbourg. If the defence of the city were to last a long time, the rations stored there would also need to last. This would be impossible if there were too many worn-out troops to be fed. Lieutenant-General Stegmann therefore decided, no matter how the situation unfolded, that the regiments under his command would evade the area being encircled and withdraw to the south.

However, the Americans had in the meantime lunged as far as the west coast of the Cotentin Peninsula. The planned withdrawal of the 77th Infantry Division would thus have to become a breakout, and, according to the report subsequently prepared by its third general staff officer, it was at 2300 hours on 17 June that the divisional units disengaged. Their objective was to reach the area to the south of the swampy terrain via Colomby, Magneville, Saint-Jacques-de-Néhou, and Saint-Lô-d'Ourville. It was not yet known that by then the US VII Corps had made such significant progress in its advance to the west that it already stood behind the flank of our 77th Infantry Division. The right wing of the infantry division therefore took an initial step back towards Orglandes, and an obstacle line was set up by the 177th Anti-Tank Battalion south of Colomby and Magneville and by the III Battalion of the 177th Motorised Artillery Regiment (under Colonel Johannes Stoltenburg) east of Saint-Jacques-de-Néhou. This would ensure that the withdrawal was shielded. Despite the danger from the air, the rear elements of the infantry division began to move by day behind this line of security. Without suffering any major casualties, they reached a position near La Haye-du-Puits. The combat troops proceeded at night. Their rear-guard units had just warded off an advance detachment of the headquarters of the US 9th Infantry Division, which had only landed on 11 June, after which the main body had set off. Unfortunately, our reconnaissance units soon reported that Saint-Jacques-de-Néhou had been occupied by the enemy, which meant that our most direct route to the south had been cut off. An infantry pioneer platoon of approximately 100 men was immediately dispatched to retake the village, but it was unable to overcome the fierce resistance of the US 39th Infantry Regiment. As a result, additional infantry and artillery forces had to be sent there, and heavy fighting ended up taking place between 0400 and 0600 hours.

With the German spearhead shattered by concentrated enemy mortar fire, there was no longer any hope that the withdrawal could be conducted undisturbed; it would have to be fought for tooth and nail.

The infantry division swung back further to the north so that it could gain enough space to reach the west coast of the peninsula and escape from the area being encircled by the enemy. As dawn broke, however, enemy fighter-bombers were able to make out the line of vehicles. Within an hour, they destroyed the remaining horse-drawn elements of the infantry division as well as many of the motor vehicles. Losses in terms of personnel were relatively low, although it was a particularly bitter blow when the divisional commander, while trying to sort out the mess of vehicles, was killed by a 2cm shell at 0600 hours only a few hundred metres to the south-east of Bricquebec. Divided into smaller groups of roughly company strength, the infantry division proceeded throughout the day on foot and reached a position approximately 4 kilometres from Barneville. It was at that moment that our men saw paratroopers of the US 82nd Airborne Division descending from the skies to occupy the town.

Storming a firmly established enemy front line without artillery or heavy weaponry would have been utterly hopeless, so Colonel Rudolf Bacherer, the commander of the 1049th Infantry Regiment and the longest-serving regimental commander in the infantry division, arranged a meeting of the leaders of the divisional units. It was 1800 hours. Most of the officers were inclined to withdraw the elements of the infantry division to Cherbourg, while others were of the view that the prospects for success were so low that it would be best to cease fighting altogether. The new and energetic divisional commander decided it would be irresponsible to allow 1,500 men to go into captivity when every man and every rifle would be needed for the establishment of the new line of resistance. With its forces concentrated once more, the battle group set off on 19 June at 0100 hours and headed south. Several Volkswagen vehicles, and even two radio cars, were silently wheeled through the first American line. By dawn, our forces were marching through villages that had already been occupied by the enemy. None of the sentries dared to open fire. They all gave way to the silent column of German troops. The signal battalion even picked up the telephone lines in the American rear area so that it could use them for its own purposes. At 1100 hours, the exhausted troops entered a narrow gully. Thick cloud cover and light rain concealed them from the enemy. They had strayed off course and were 5 kilometres further to the west than intended. An American encampment lay only 500 metres away! Since our troops lacked the strength to march further that afternoon, a small number of guards were posted while the rest of our men slept for a few hours.

Enemy reconnaissance aircraft must have eventually discovered the rest area, for American troops were soon assembling in readiness to launch an attack. The battle group retreated a few kilometres, made a sidestep, and requested by radio that the 243rd Infantry Division open the American obstacle line between Portbail and Doville. The opening was created at Villot instead, and an enemy position was taken by surprise and overrun by some German assault guns that had approached from behind. There still existed the danger that everything would fail at the Ollande River, but the I Battalion of the German 1050th Infantry Regiment stormed the enemy-occupied bridge, annihilated the II Battalion of the US 47th Infantry Regiment, and reached safety further to the south not only with all its wounded but also with 12 captured Jeeps and approximately 250 prisoners of war.

The breakout had succeeded. It was a glorious chapter of the fighting in Normandy. By 1400 hours on 20 June, the three days of uncertainty had come to an end. Contact had been established with the battle group that had been sent by the 243rd Infantry Division (by then under the command of Colonel Bernhard Klosterkemper). The troops assembled in the area between Angoville-sur-Ay and Saint-German-sur-Ay, and Colonel Bacherer was awarded the Knight's Cross of the Iron Cross with Oak Leaves.

Smaller groups of German troops fought their way along the beach of the west coast of the peninsula at low tide in the days that followed. They passed the camps that had been set up for French civilian refugees by mayors whose villages had become sites of battle.

While the remains of our divisions were organised into individual battle groups, the 353rd Infantry Division was approaching along the Coutances–Périers road. This new formation would become the backbone of the LXXXIV Army Corps in the fighting that followed.

Several American formations pivoted to the north to advance on Cherbourg. Those that remained on the southern side of the corridor were reorganised, replenished with fresh men and equipment, and ordered to dig in. The weather was bad, and the fighting died down for a few days. This allowed time for the strengthening of the German defensive line, which ran as follows: the hills near La Meauffe–the west bank of the Vire through Cavigny–the southern side of the Canal de Vire et Taute–Graignes–Sainteny–the western side of the Prairies Marécageuses de Gorges–Saint-Jores–the southern side of the Bois de Limors–the southern side of the Prairies Marécageuses–Saint-Sauveur-de-Pierrepont–the northern side of the railway line–the west coast at Saint-Lô-d'Ourville.

It was in this situation that Lieutenant-General Dietrich von Choltitz assumed command of the army corps, for General Wilhelm Fahrmbacher, at his own request, had been relieved on 20 June. The task to be carried out by the new commander was nothing to be envied. With tremendous effort and in rather a makeshift manner, he saw to the reorganisation of the battered divisions, their commands, and their means of supply. The conduct of operations to the north, near Cherbourg, lay outside his area of responsibility. The only reserves at his disposal, aside from the approaching 353rd Infantry Division, were the 797th Georgian Battalion in Coutances, the 521st Security Battalion in Granville, and, much further back, the 8th Werfer Brigade immediately to the east of Vire.

Lieutenant-General von Choltitz was a man who had distinguished himself as a field commander. He came from a family that had produced senior military officers and civil servants for generations. His career was filled with many highlights. In 1940, as a battalion commander in the 16th Air Landing Regiment (which had been formed in Oldenburg), Choltitz had seized the air base and bridges in Rotterdam and had held on to them for the bulk of the advancing German forces. In Crimea in 1942, his 16th Infantry Regiment had been the first formation to enter Sevastopol. In 1944, before arriving in Normandy, he had commanded the LXXVI Panzer Corps in the fighting around the Nettuno beachhead in Italy.

While General Marcks had always been cool, calm, and collected, Lieutenant-General von Choltitz was of a warm and impulsive temperament. He possessed diplomatic skill coupled with a remarkable gift for speaking with young officers and men and confidently doing what needed to be done. He was an ideal senior officer who overcame many concerns at the front with his dry, grim sense of humour and who enjoyed a comradely relationship with his divisional commanders. If tension arose, it was because of the urgent need to patch up the front everywhere at once and thus the occasional order was issued directly to smaller units. He always strove to base his decisions on good reasoning, and he never minced words when dealing with his superiors.

He was fully aware of the difficulties of the task before him. The situation unfolding on the Cotentin Peninsula somewhat resembled what had taken place near Nettuno. His level-headed assessment of the situation was as follows: 'The front must be held so that the political leadership, in the most favourable situation possible, has the time and the opportunity to make decisions.'

Although there could be no question that his services to the Fatherland were second to none, Choltitz would end up being made the scapegoat for the successful breakthrough of the Americans at Avranches on 29 July. He was blamed for the consequences of a withdrawal to the southeast that had been ordered by the Seventh Army, even though he had objected to this course of action beforehand. He was nonetheless, after a brief visit to the Führer's headquarters, promoted to general of infantry and appointed as military governor of Greater Paris a few days later. As fate would have it, he would spare the French capital destruction, just as General Marcks had done in 1940. For this reason, he is highly regarded in France today.

The fall of Cherbourg

On the Cherbourg front, the left wing of the Montebourg–Quinéville defensive position had been in a severely weakened state since 18 June. This position was held by Battle Group Rohrbach, which was composed of elements of the 729th and 739th Infantry Regiments. Lieutenant-General von Schlieben ordered the battle group and other isolated elements to retreat to the line connecting Valognes, the upper course of the Douve, Couville, and the west coast of the peninsula at Cap de Flamanville. The Americans pursued our retreat only hesitantly to begin with. The US VII Corps sent its 4th Infantry Division towards Montebourg, its 79th Infantry Division towards Valognes, and its 9th Infantry Division towards Bricquebec. By 21 June, the Americans had reached a position outside Cherbourg, and it was there that the fighting increased in intensity. The 191st Pioneer Battalion (subordinate to the 91st Air Landing Division) had already been mentioned in the Wehrmacht communiqué on 17 June for its role in the preparation of defensive fortifications.

On the evening of 21 June, the commander of the US VII Corps, Major General J. Lawton Collins, issued an ultimatum by radio and via a military negotiator. The headquarters of the LXXXIV Army Corps listened to the ultimatum. It was broadcast in German and repeated in French, Polish, and Russian in order to persuade ethnic-only (i.e. non-citizen) Germans as well as eastern troops and French labourers to lay down their arms or put down their tools. The ultimatum stated that the harbour had been cut off, that the situation of the battle group was without hope, and that the deadline for surrendering would be 0900 hours on 22 June. Lieutenant-General von Schlieben did not bother with a response. He knew that he had to tie down enemy forces for as long as possible and that he had to see to the complete destruction of the harbour installations.

An extensive aerial bombardment marked the commencement of the assault on Cherbourg. The nature of the front before the city requires some explanation. Only in the few weeks leading up to the invasion of Normandy had the city been fortified. The work had been done with haste and in a makeshift fashion. As a result, parts of the front existed only on paper. Cherbourg stood facing the sea and had not been built up inland. General Marcks had repeatedly pointed out the vulnerability of this 'soft belly'. We were aware of how the British had paid the price for a similar state of vulnerability when Singapore fell to the Japanese in 1942. However, the army corps had been deprived of much of the concrete it needed for the sake of the nearby V-1 launch site. Our trenches

THE BATTLE OF CHERBOURG (7–26 JUNE 1944) • 59

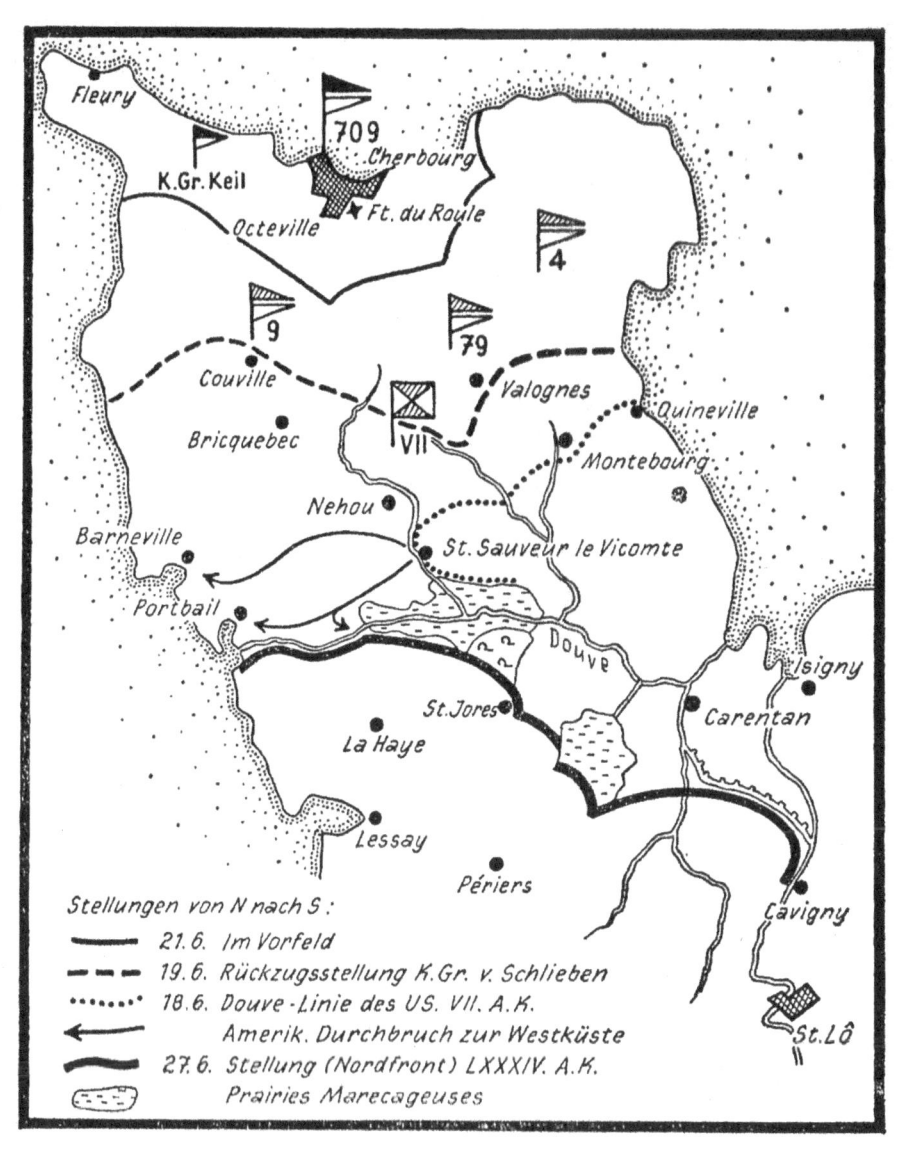

Map 7: The front before Cherbourg

were often lacking wire obstacles in front of them, and many shelters were covered by nothing more than a layer of tree trunks. The terrain was hilly, crisscrossed with valleys and dotted with wooded areas, which meant that it was not always possible to see the enemy.

Every effort was made to increase the strength of our companies or platoons to approximately 80 men: the 17th Machine Gun Battalion was split up into smaller units, and personnel were drawn from the Reich Labour Service (RAD), flak troops, Luftwaffe signal troops, supply troops, and veterinary companies. However, aside from the 18-year-olds of the RAD, the new personnel were of little use: they lacked training and were psychologically ill-prepared for the severe challenges of the battlefield.

In a subsequent report on the fighting in which the Hessian-Thuringian 919th Grenadier Regiment had been involved, Lieutenant-Colonel Günther Keil described the characteristics of the conduct of battle of the Americans. Any attack by enemy tanks on a strongpoint, no matter how weak it had become, would be preceded by an air raid carried out by approximately 50 aircraft. A sudden concentration of mortar fire would take place after that and would be coordinated with the advance of an assault detachment. This assault detachment would be equipped with radiotelephones and would immediately report any success or failure at once. Before the German company commander could be informed by messenger of anything that had happened, the enemy assault detachment would call for an attack by stronger forces. These forces would seize the German position and would establish an all-round defence prior to the commencement of any weak German counter-attack. It was under these difficult circumstances that our regimental headquarters had to conduct operations. Orderly officers had to be dispatched on motorcycles to make up for the failure of telephone lines, but it was a full hour before the enemy situation had been clarified. The preparation of counter-measures took another hour due to the influence of enemy aircraft and artillery. During that time, the situation had changed considerably, and it was only ever bad news.

The enemy reached the outskirts of the city at Octeville on 24 June. Bombs fell nonstop on our forts and anti-aircraft gun emplacements, and our signal communications were largely interrupted. The inadequately armed and equipped Russian volunteers did not hold out for long, and we could see that the Americans were assembling their tanks and bringing their guns into position immediately to the south-east of the city.

The situation rapidly came to a head on 25 June. The Fort du Roule, in the southern part of Cherbourg, fell at noon. It had until then been able to exert its influence on the enemy routes of advance, but now the Americans had moved beyond it. Nothing else stood in their way. Our forces were confronted with an impossible task, with defensive obstacles lacking in the suburbs, bombs falling on the city centre, and naval artillery firing from the sea. We were losing many of our best young officers, and the chaotic state of the civilian authorities did little to alleviate the situation.

A medical officer from the naval hospital, accompanied by a captured lieutenant of the USAAF, had gone through the lines of the US 9th Infantry Division that morning. He reported that the hospital had been damaged and requested medicine and plasma for wounded prisoners of war. He returned with a written demand, to be delivered to Lieutenant-General von Schlieben, that the German forces cease hostilities. The lieutenant-general rejected this demand, after which he radioed his superiors:

> Where is the Luftwaffe? Where are our fast attack craft? The enemy possesses overwhelming materiel and aerial superiority. Most of our batteries are out of ammunition or have been destroyed. Our units are worn out and have been pushed back into a small area between the enemy and the sea. The harbour installations and anything else of importance have been blown up. The loss of the city is inevitable. The enemy has already infiltrated its periphery. There are 2,000 wounded who are unable to be transported to safety. Given the overall situation and our lack of effective weaponry, is it necessary that our remaining forces be annihilated? Orders required urgently.

The reply from the commander of Army Group B, Field Marshal Rommel, was received at 1548 hours: 'In accordance with the directive issued by the Führer, you must fight to the bitter end.'

The struggle dissolved into a number of skirmishes that were no longer centrally controlled. Naval Coastal Batteries Blankenese, Hamburg, Brommy, and York put up tough resistance. The Hamburg battery, under the command of Lieutenant Rudi Gelbhaar, sank two Cumberland-class cruisers. The last act of destruction took place on 27 June when the docks by Fort du Homet were blown up. The harbour commandant, Captain Hermann Witt, made use of a sailing yacht and several rowboats to transfer his command post to Fort West and to lay a new minefield.

The city centre, and with it the command post of the battle group, were taken in close combat on 26 June. The last radio message from Cherbourg had been sent the evening before, at 2010 hours: 'The final fight has broken out. The lieutenant-general is alongside his troops.' The headquarters of the Seventh Army had radioed its reply: 'We are with you!' On the morning of 26 June, the enemy came to within a hundred metres of the command bunker. Schlieben and the officers of the headquarters of the battle group, armed only with infantry weapons, defended the entrances and fought well into the afternoon. The fire from enemy tanks, mortars, and machine guns eventually compelled them to take cover. The Americans then threw explosive devices into the ventilation shaft, which stopped the air supply from working and threatened to suffocate the many who were wounded. Further resistance would be futile and irresponsible. Cherbourg had fallen.

The fighting continued a little longer on the Jobourg Peninsula, which lay to the north-west of Cherbourg's harbour. This area had been nicknamed 'Intelligence Peninsula' due to the mass of signal communication equipment that had been set up there by the navy and the Luftwaffe for the observation of the southern coast of England. Its defence was the responsibility of Battle Group Keil. This formation comprised the headquarters and II Battalion of the 919th Infantry Regiment, elements of the 922nd Infantry Regiment (of the 243rd Infantry Division), the assault battalion of the Seventh Army, the light flak battalion of the 25th Flak Regiment, two artillery battalions, and several smaller units. The state of telephone communications with the Channel Islands was good, which meant that the battle group remained in contact with the Seventh Army until the end of the month, when it could hold out no longer.

It need not be said how Lieutenant-General von Choltitz and the others at the headquarters of the army corps felt about the news of the fall of Cherbourg. The daily propaganda leaflet produced by the enemy,

Nachrichten für die Truppe, emphasised the significance of the event. On the front side of the issue that covered this American victory were two photographs: the first depicted Lieutenant-General Karl-Wilhelm von Schlieben and Rear Admiral Walter Hennecke being questioned by an interpreter in the presence of US Major General J. Lawton Collins; the second showed the officers of the headquarters of the 709th Infantry Division, all of them known to us and now taken prisoner, boarding a ship bound for England.

Tragically, the naval port for which four divisions had been put on the line was not vital for the enemy at that stage. Although it would be important to him in the future, he had for now been able to safeguard the flow of supplies to his ever-growing ground forces by means that were not yet known to us.

The invasion never would have been a success without the enormous contribution made by Allied science and technology. The sheer, inexhaustible economic power of two empires supported and maximised this contribution. Temporary portable harbours known as Mulberry harbours were prefabricated in England, towed in sections across the English Channel, and assembled off the coast of the Cotentin Peninsula by British pioneer and naval personnel as well as American naval construction units. Vast stretches of water were thereby rapidly transformed into temporary harbours whose floating piers rose and fell with the ebb and flow of the sea. Block ships were scuttled to act as simple breakwaters, creating relatively sheltered areas of shallow water where special vessels could ride at anchor. From 7 June, the enemy brought roughly 2,000 motor vehicles of all types and about 12,000 tonnes of supplies into Normandy every day.

The landing craft were the result of years of development and construction. They had been tested in home waters, employed for the landings in Madagascar, North Africa, and Italy, and, based on the experiences that had been gained, constantly improved. They had to fulfil a number of fundamental requirements, including long range, high speed, and thus the possibility of being self-propelled rather than just towed. Also important were versatility in the attack, the provision of artillery close support, the supply of equipment, and, in the case of the newest type of Landing Craft Tank (LCT), the attachment of a bow door.

Another important invention was called Pipeline Under the Ocean (PLUTO), which enabled the daily delivery of 4.5 million litres of fuel to Normandy and therefore the full and continuous operational readiness of Allied tanks and aircraft. On 19 June, a violent storm had severely damaged the artificial harbour in the northern American landing zone. The repair of Cherbourg's harbour would reduce the impact of any further storms, so 25,000 pioneers worked feverishly for weeks to make the piers, cranes, and warehouses capable of being used once more. That repair work was done by September 1944, even if in a somewhat makeshift fashion to begin with, and this allowed men, materiel, and even whole goods trains to be ferried from southern England to Normandy from then on.

In its war diary on 27 June 1944, OB West recorded its assessment of the probable development of the situation:

> The American forces in the vicinity of Cherbourg have become available and will be able, in part from 28 June and in whole from about 30 June, to be committed to the Carentan–Portbail sector. It can therefore be expected that the offensive against the northern front of the LXXXIV Army Corps will resume no later than the beginning of July. The enemy will most likely place the point of main effort of his attack near Carentan and will presumably advance from there in the direction of Coutances in order to cut off German forces further to the north.

CHAPTER 3

The breakthrough of the Americans (26 June–31 July 1944)

The fighting in the six weeks from 18 June, when the Americans reached the west coast at Barneville, to 31 July 1944, when the Americans infiltrated Avranches in preparation for the advance deep into northern France, constantly went back and forth and was filled with a number of individual strikes, holding attacks, and defensive actions conducted by both sides. Given the precise coordination of the operations conducted by the British and the Americans, it was the German forces that ultimately had to yield ground.

It had been relatively quiet on the northern front of the LXXXIV Army Corps while the struggle for Cherbourg had been underway. In the sector that stretched from Vire to the coast, the US First Army had set up a defensive position, digging in and regrouping on its right wing in particular. Enemy aircraft were kept on the ground due not only to the period of poor weather that had set in but also to the severe wear and tear that had resulted from their extensive use in the first few weeks of the invasion.

If, during this pause in the fighting, the OKW had abandoned its belief that a larger landing would take place in the Pas-de-Calais and had made multiple divisions and panzer formations from the coastal sector between Calais and Le Havre available for a counter-attack, there would have been good prospects of success. The temporary absence of enemy bombers and fighter-bombers would have made the movement of reserves easier, proof of which is provided by the almost trouble-free arrival of the 353rd Infantry Division (Lieutenant-General Paul Mahlmann) from

Brittany. This division, headquartered in La Tringale near Périers, was placed under the command of the army corps on 18 June, and it assumed responsibility for the vital central sector and remained the backbone of the army corps in the period that followed.

The Allies occupied a narrow area at that time. They were held at bay by reasonably strong German lines and had neither the ability to conduct extensive operational movements nor the possibility to fully exploit their superiority in men and materiel. Although they had penetrated the Atlantic Wall, our defensive efforts prevented them from lunging forward and achieving a decisive victory.

It could therefore be expected that the immediate objective of the Allies would be to fully build up their invasion armies. This would require that they fight hard to create an assembly area for 30 to 40 divisions. They were very much in danger of becoming stuck in a small beachhead and having to go over to the defensive, so their intention could be nothing other than to break out of the narrow area they currently occupied and advance far into northern France.

The fundamental principle adhered to by the enemy in his conduct of battle was 'safety first'. He shied away from any risk. His planning for the invasion was an example of strategic excellence, and his ability to supply the invasion force demonstrated organisational brilliance, yet he tended to go into too much detail when issuing operational commands. The lower levels of command closely followed the orders they had been given and displayed barely any degree of personal initiative. They moved forward carefully and lacked the agility required to properly exploit favourable opportunities. We observed time and again how the enemy would stay put once he had reached his objective of the day. He exercised considerable restraint and cautiously reassembled his forces for the continuation of the attack the following day. The various branches of his armed forces worked effectively with one another, which was mainly a result of the overwhelming aerial superiority he enjoyed. Nevertheless, confronted with fierce German resistance, his progress was slow and even awkward to begin with.

A kind of positional warfare prevailed in the months of June and July. The enemy sought to push his way through the pastureland of the wooded countryside and along the valley of the Orne near Caen in order to reach open terrain. Probing the front in multiple locations, he sometimes conducted major attacks and holding attacks, and at other times became embroiled in unidirectional or multidirectional skirmishes. Caen would become a real nightmare for Montgomery. Given the superiority of his units in terms of materiel, his efforts there must be regarded as a defeat in the end. The metre-by-metre offensive carried out by the British was bitterly criticised in their homeland. A series of costly attacks had been unleashed. At Caumont, in front of Hill 112, and to the south of Caen, the enemy sacrificed one battalion after another and fired hundreds of thousands of shells so that he could seize dominant positions. British and Canadian troops bore the main burden of the first phase of this fighting. They suffered the heaviest casualties and experienced serious setbacks. Only when the Americans broke through the western wing of the German defensive position did the positional warfare in Normandy develop into mobile warfare in France. It was time for the armoured formations of the US Third Army, commanded by Lieutenant General George S. Patton, to take the field.

Time was in fact running out for the enemy. He needed to secure major harbours for the long-term supply of his ground forces, as the Mulberry harbours, lacking in the large installations to be found in military ports, would be useless after the early autumn. Furthermore, not to be underestimated was the political value of a breakout by the enemy deep into France. It would have had a positive effect on public opinion in southern England and would have been watched eagerly not only by the French but also by the entire world. The constant bombardment of London and southern England with V-1 flying bombs had led to the evacuation of large numbers of civilians. The people of England wanted this threat and the strain on the nerves associated with it to come to an end, and this required that the V-1 launch sites be captured as soon as possible. That this was a primary objective of the enemy was clearly revealed by some of the correspondence of his that fell into our hands.

In all the measures that they took, the Allies possessed the inestimable advantage of being able to quickly concentrate their fully motorised divisions for an attack. They probed our defences and were able to increase the momentum of their initial successes through the immediate employment of reserves. All our counter-thrusts were intercepted. Several enemy formations composed of armoured, artillery, and pioneer units arrived as reinforcements. They enabled the Allies to create points of main effort without having to go through the time-consuming process of scraping together elements of units or having to settle for attack fronts of limited strength and width. The appearance of these reinforcements nevertheless made it easier for us to discern the intentions of the enemy.

Although German forces in the West had achieved the incredible in the past, years of depletion put them at an immediate disadvantage against the full-strength enemy in Normandy. In view of the considerable demands placed on our limited forces and the bit-by-bit release of reinforcements for Normandy, we had to resort, by necessity, to a system of expediencies and tactical patchwork. The difficulty of the situation meant that any small units that arrived often had to be committed at once to crisis sectors of the front before they had even been allocated to our divisions. This unfortunate shredding of our formations negatively impacted the morale of our troops, with valuable pioneer units employed as infantry. In a period of three months, only one of the weakened divisions of the LXXXIV Army Corps – the 77th Infantry Division – was withdrawn from the front to be refreshed and refitted. The others were burned to ashes.

Aside from the fact that the enemy ground forces received naval and aerial support, something that our ground forces lacked, we found that, from the beginning of July, the strength of those enemy ground forces started to greatly outweigh our power of resistance.

The organisation of our forces along the entire invasion front on the morning of 21 June 1944 was as follows:

A. Opposing the British sector
   I. Panzer Group West
      1. LXXXVI Army Corps (Cabourg–Troarn–Bourguébus) (headquarters in Gerrots)
         (a) 711th Infantry Division (Glanville)
         (b) 346th Infantry Division (Saint-Léger)
         (c) 7th Werfer Brigade
         (d) Battle Group Luck

2. I SS Panzer Corps (valley of the Orne near Caen–Tilly-sur-Seulles–valley of the Aure
   (a) 21st Panzer Division
   (b) 12th SS Panzer Division Hitlerjugend
   (c) Panzer Lehr Division
II. Seventh Army
   3. XXXXVII Panzer Corps (Caumont)
      (a) 2nd SS Panzer Division Das Reich
      (b) Reconnaissance battalion of the 17th SS Panzer Grenadier Division Götz von Berlichingen
B. Opposing the American sector
   4. II Parachute Corps (Forêt de Cerisy–Saint-Lô–Pont-Hébert)
      (a) 3rd Parachute Division (Saint-Armand)
      (b) Elements of the 353rd Infantry Division
      (c) 30th Mobile Brigade
      (d) A battle group of the 352nd Infantry Division
   5. LXXXIV Army Corps (left bank of the Vire–Prairies Marécageuses–west coast) (headquarters in Saint-Sauveur-Lendelin)
      (a) 17th SS Panzer Grenadier Division Götz von Berlichingen with the 635th Eastern Battalion, a battle group of the 275th Infantry Division, and the assault battalion of the Seventh Army
      (b) 6th Parachute Regiment
      (c) 353rd Infantry Division
      (d) Battle groups from the 77th, 243rd, and 265th Infantry Divisions

After an unsuccessful attack by the British at Villers-Bocage on 25 June, a new attack was launched by the British VIII Corps three days later from the vicinity of Tilly-sur-Seulles. It was the second attempt to outflank Caen from the south-west and to compel German forces in the city to retreat. The territorial gain of the enemy initially amounted to no more than a narrow salient approximately four kilometres in depth, but it expanded into a strong bridgehead across the Odon and the fighting there became particularly fierce. The objective of the enemy was to secure the high ground between the Odon and the Orne and, from there, to take Caen from the rear. This dangerous situation was overcome on 29 June by the II SS Panzer Corps (SS-General Paul Hausser with the 9th SS Panzer Division Hohenstaufen and 10th SS Panzer Division Frundsberg), in conjunction with the 21st Panzer Division (which struck the British bridgehead from the east). Both formations had just arrived from Poland and were well equipped. The German thrust against the British flank was led by approximately 150 tanks, and its objective was ambitious. Aside from recapturing the ground that had been lost, our tanks were supposed to lunge well beyond the Caen–Bayeux road as far as the coast. Unfortunately, clear blue skies permitted extensive enemy aerial activity and thereby delayed the completion of our preparations until 1800 hours. The concentrated fire of the three branches of the British armed forces, especially that of the heavy naval units, prevented our forces from achieving full success. Nevertheless, in the vicinity of Gavrus, the II SS Panzer Corps hurled the British off the high ground that lay to the east of the Orne and thus dashed Montgomery's hopes of taking Caen for quite some time. In order to lighten the load for the British, the Americans expanded their sector of the front from the beginning of July so that it stretched as far as the Balleroy–Caumont area. This meant that British forces no longer stood opposite the LXXXIV Army Corps. Only in the days of the battle of the Falaise pocket would there be a renewed clash between British forces and the army corps.

A second major attack was launched by the British on 4 July. Enemy artillery fire in the Tilly–Caumont sector aimed to rip open the left wing of Panzer Group West: 3,500 rounds were fired in less than two hours. The main line of advance would be in the direction of Villers-Bocage, yet we had only two companies to defend this sector to begin with. The struggle lasted for days. Air raids conducted by 500 heavy bombers helped the British I Corps make progress against the battered formations of the 21st Panzer Division, 12th SS Panzer Division Hitlerjugend, and 16th Luftwaffe Field Division. By 9 July, Caen, aside from the suburbs to the south of the Orne, had been occupied by the enemy. It had taken Montgomery more than one month to push forward 12 kilometres, even though this was the distance that, according to the Allied operational

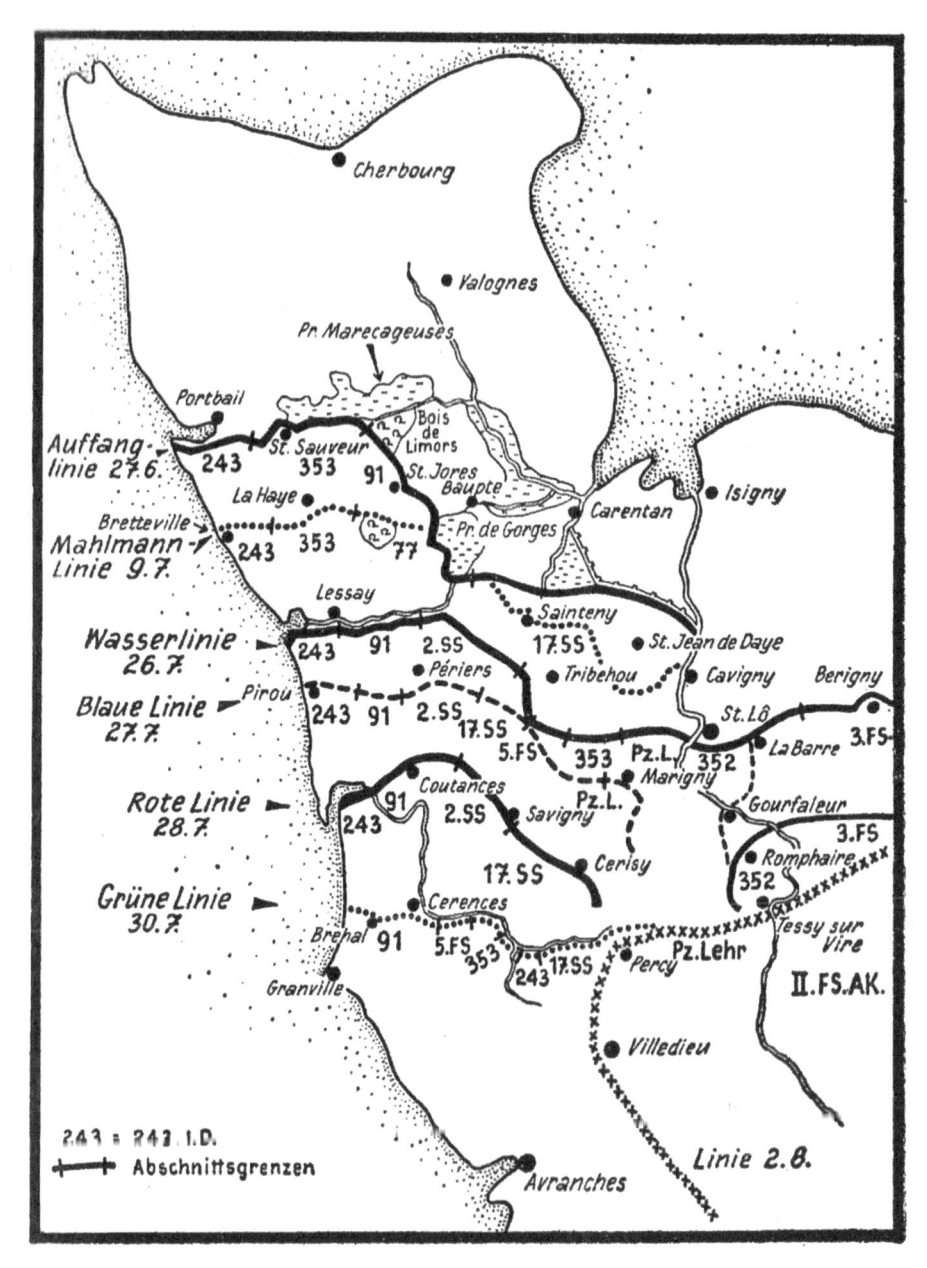

THE BREAKTHROUGH OF THE AMERICANS (26 JUNE–31 JULY 1944) • 71

Map 8: The combat zone of the LXXXIV Army Corps from 27 June 1944 until 2 August 1944

plan, was supposed to have been covered on the very first day of the landings. Enemy area bombing may have destroyed our positions, but the enormous craters that had been left behind made it difficult for the British tanks to make progress. It was for this reason that the enemy subsequently made use of lighter bombs, whose blast effect was nonetheless powerful and directed horizontally. The fighting for control of Carpiquet Airfield went back and forth until 11 July. The surrounding terrain changed hands multiple times, and it was there that units of the 12th SS Panzer Division Hitlerjugend wiped out the French-Canadian Régiment de la Chaudière (of the Canadian 3rd Infantry Division).

From 3 July, the Americans, in an effort to assist the British, struck the northern front of the LXXXIV Army Corps in the vicinity of La Haye-du-Puits, near the Forêt de Mont-Castre. Weak German security units had been stationed in the forest in the immediate proximity of Mont Castre when the US First Army commenced its offensive, and they were overrun after the intensive preparatory fire of enemy artillery. The main reason for our defeat there was the poor conduct of Eastern Regiment Bunyachenko.

So that its front could be strengthened, the LXXXIV Army Corps was allocated the 15th Parachute Regiment. Commanded by Colonel Kurt Gröschke, this regiment had come from the 5th Parachute Division and was now subordinated to the 77th Infantry Division. Although its personnel predominantly comprised young recruits with little training, the parachute regiment fought with distinction. It retook some of the forest terrain from the determined Texans of the US 90th Infantry Division, even though observation aircraft aided enemy artillery units and despite dozens of enemy fighter-bombers circling over the forest with its historic Camp de César. The parachute regiment later had to withdraw from its hastily dug foxholes, but it did so with the greatest of resistance and limited the depth of penetration of what was supposed to be a major thrust by the enemy to 200 metres! Fortunately, the terrain made it difficult for an attack to be carried out with tanks. Given that the American infantry formations were unable to make much progress without the support of tanks, German defensive efforts involved the concentration of forces in positions that might be vulnerable to an attack by tanks and the employment of artillery fire and reconnaissance units in other locations that were otherwise unoccupied. The fighting near Mont Castre was some of the most bitter that took place in the hedgerow countryside of Normandy.

It required tremendous effort on the part of the third general staff officer of the army corps to develop a clear picture of what the enemy was up to. A few days went by before he could deliver his report to General von Choltitz:

> The US VIII Corps is regrouping. It seems that the US 82nd Airborne Division has been relieved, as it has not been seen at the front for several days. A prisoner of war has stated that the airborne division has been sent back to southern England for reorganisation. The combat zone for which it had been responsible has been taken over by the recently arrived US 8th Infantry Division. Correspondence belonging to the US 83rd Infantry Division was seized from an army postal officer who had fallen on the battlefield, and it reveals that this formation has also just recently arrived in Normandy. Changes have likewise taken place in the sector on the west bank of the Vire. The enemy has shifted his sector boundaries and reduced the size of his attack sectors by moving the US 1st Infantry Division from the Caumont front to the area south of the Canal de Vire et Taute.

For the time being, it was the 353rd Infantry Division that had to resist most of the southward pressure applied by the enemy. It held the 15-kilometre Lithaire–Neufmesnil sector, which lay to the north of La Haye-du-Puits and Montgardon, with only four infantry battalions and two artillery battalions. The urgency of the situation demanded that the infantry division be broken up and that each regiment hand over a battalion to its neighbour. Heavy fighting unfolded around the town of La Haye-du-Puits, which was defended by the 353rd Pioneer Battalion. Only once this formation had been reduced to approximately 40 men were the Americans able to push through the town to its southern outskirts.

In honour of the commander of the 353rd Infantry Division, the LXXXIV Army Corps referred to the front that had been established by 9 July as the Mahlmann Line: Cavigny (12 kilometres north of Saint-Lô)–Le Dézert–the Canal de Vire et Taute at a point north of Graignes–Sainteny–western edge of the Prairies Marécageuses de Gorges–northern edge of the Forêt de Mont-Castre–southern outskirts of La Haye-du-Puits–Bretteville–west coast. On the night of 13/14 July,

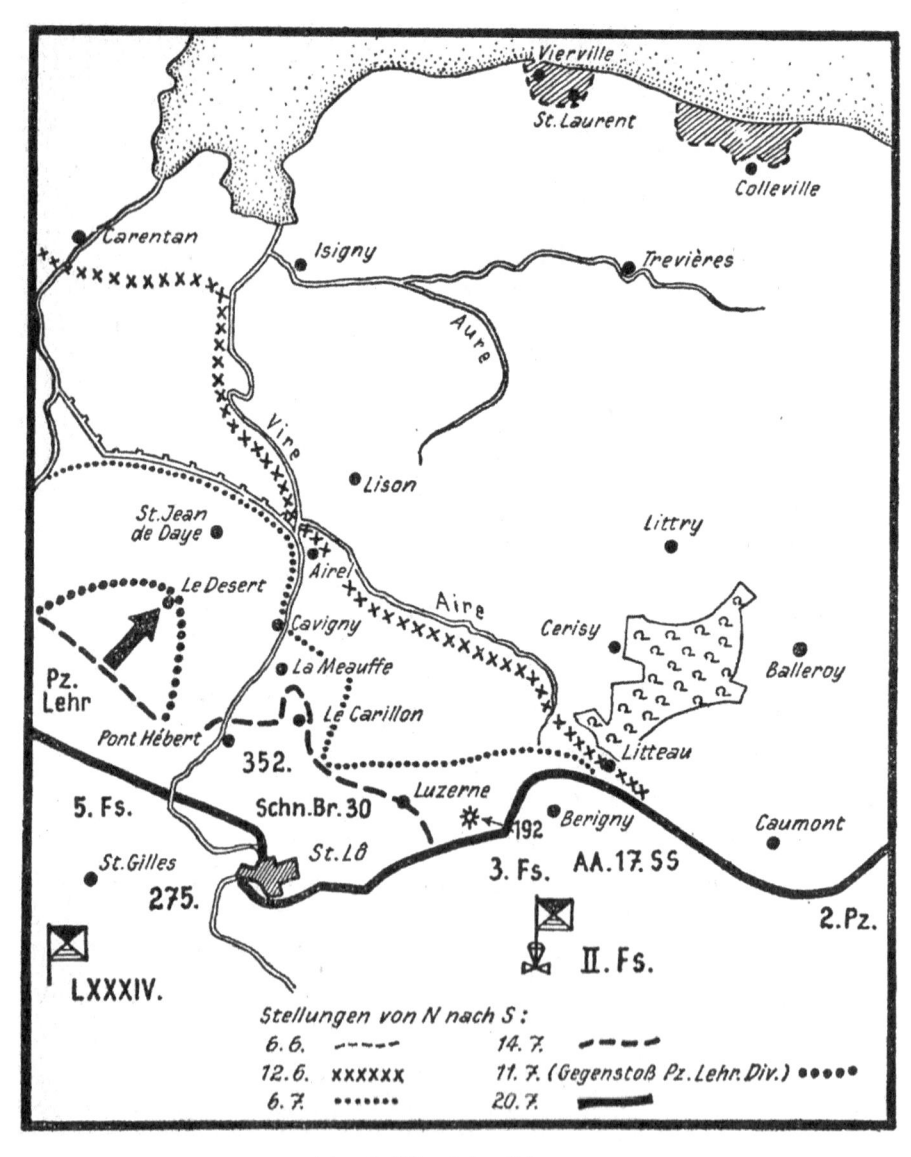

Map 9: The Saint-Lô sector

the withdrawal to the so-called Water Position was carried out. Ten days later, the infantry division, whose strength by then amounted to only about 2,000 men, moved to the right to the area north-west of Marigny.

In the meantime, in the central sector of the LXXXIV Army Corps, the 17th SS Panzer Grenadier Division Götz von Berlichingen and Battle Group Heinz (of the 275th Infantry Division) clashed with the US XIX Corps. The usual ratio of forces applied here as well, in a combat zone encompassing the marshland of the Canal de Vire et Taute.

The landscape was vast and filled not only with dams and ponds but also with a number of narrow and irregularly laid-out drainage ditches. The barely flowing streams flooded the meadows even when there was light rain. The roads, useful only for farming activities, were difficult to navigate. The successful conduct of an armoured attack by either side was dependent on the employment of a couple of dry routes that ran through gently undulating ranges of hills. The eastern route was the road connecting Carentan, Saint-Jean-de-Daye, and Pont-Hébert, while the western road, lying only 2 kilometres away from the completely impassable Prairies Marécageuses de Gorges, was that connecting Carentan, Sainteny, and Périers. Extensive combat in the northern part of the Prairies Marécageuses de Gorges could be ruled out, so the area, monitored only by outposts, became an arena for the contest between snipers. The men of the 37th SS Panzer Grenadier Regiment were specialists in this type of secret war. Eyes squinting, they waited between hedges and in scattered farms for any kind of movement. A shot would ring out across no man's land, and then a deceptive silence would reign once more. German reconnaissance activity led to the capture of some prisoners, enabling the third general staff officer of the 17th SS Panzer Grenadier Division Götz von Berlichingen, SS-Captain Hans-Wedigo von Le Coq, to contribute valuable intelligence regarding the enemy situation.

On 7 July, the US 30th Infantry Division launched a surprise attack from the right bank of the Vire against the flank of the 17th SS Panzer Grenadier Division Götz von Berlichingen. The bulk of the forces of this SS formation had destroyed the bridges over the Vire and mined the banks of the river before withdrawing to Tribehou. Only a few weak elements of the SS formation remained near the river. The Americans crossed the river at 0430 hours at Saint-Fromond, which lay immediately to the south of the confluence of this river and the Canal de Vire et Taute, by making use of a hastily repaired bridge. A second crossing point was set up through the employment of boats. In the dark and misty weather, visibility was poor for the German artillery units, and this made it possible for the enemy battle group to envelop two SS regiments and several special SS units and to push as far as Saint-Jean-de-Daye. This main thrust was supported by a holding attack from the north across the mined banks of the canal. It is worth mentioning that the Americans had reached the north bank of the canal on 17 June, a few days after the fall of Carentan, yet three weeks had gone by since then without the enemy advancing any further.

After the capture of Saint-Jean-de-Daye, the enemy pressed towards Le Dézert. The German forces in the salient around Graignes and Le Port des Planques were unable to disengage from the enemy holding attack quickly enough, and the result was that many of the troops of the 38th SS Panzer Grenadier Regiment and 639th Eastern Battalion were taken prisoner. In the days that followed, the US 3rd Armored Division, maintaining a course parallel to the Vire, drove to the south. The only reserves at our disposal were the 30th Mobile Brigade and a parachute battalion, so the enemy was able to expand his breakthrough area around Saint-Jean-de-Daye such that it extended 3 kilometres along the river as far as the high ground of Pont-Hébert. This meant that Saint-Lô was now in imminent danger of being captured.

German counteractions consisted of two panzer attacks. The first was carried out by the 2nd SS Panzer Division Das Reich, which on D-Day had been in the vicinity of Toulouse in southern France. It now stormed forward from Hill 32, which lay halfway between Saint-Jean-de-Daye and Pont-Hébert, and the heaviest clash took place in the afternoon at Château de la Mare, near Cavigny. An American battalion was routed there, its men abandoning their vehicles and fleeing. The statements obtained from prisoners of war confirmed that this had been a battalion of the US 120th Infantry Regiment (of the US 30th Infantry Division). The concentrated fire of the enemy's medium and heavy artillery meant that the German success could not last for long. More than 12,000 rounds rained down and denied the SS panzer division the ability to make further progress. The respite that the attack had achieved was therefore most brief.

The LXXXIV Army Corps pinned its hopes on the counter-attack to be launched by the Panzer Lehr Division (Lieutenant-General Fritz Bayerlein) on 11 July. Formed from the training units of the schools of the panzer troops, the Panzer Lehr Division was an elite formation, although it had already been engaged in fierce fighting against the British for four weeks in the vicinity of Tilly-sur-Seulles and had in the process been reduced in strength by approximately 10,000 men. Twenty-five per cent of its forces still stood near Tilly-sur-Seulles, but the rest were to conduct an attack to the north-east from the line connecting Pont-Hébert and Le Hommet. The right spearhead, comprising the 902nd Panzer Grenadier Regiment and about 20 tanks, would carry out a frontal strike against the US 90th Infantry Division (of the US XIX Corps), while the left spearhead, made up of the 901st Panzer Grenadier Regiment, two anti-tank companies, and about 12 tanks, would hit the deep flank of the US 30th Infantry Division (of the US VII Corps). Most of the fighting raged around the village of Le Dézert. It was there, on the boundary between the two enemy corps, that the counter-thrust made the most progress. A full success would have resulted in all the enemy units that had pressed forward on the left bank of the Vire being cut off or compelled to conduct a hasty withdrawal across the river.

The German attack had put the Americans in a state of confusion. By 0600 hours, our tanks had advanced approximately three kilometres behind the enemy lines. Two battalion command posts had been overrun, elements of the US 39th Infantry Regiment (of the US 9th Infantry Division) had been encircled, and several prisoners of war had been taken. The enemy rapidly hurled multiple anti-tank units and elements of his 2nd Armored Division into the to and fro battle. Our tanks fought against the enemy vehicles, often at distances of only 150 metres, in dense orchards and on sunken roads, but they were soon struck by heavy artillery fire, while the accompanying grenadier troops were forced to take cover against enemy fighter-bombers. The counter-thrust therefore lost its momentum. The cramped combat zone and the difficulty in observing the effectiveness of our weaponry meant that our tanks were unable to fully exploit their superior range of fire. By 1600 hours, the operation, despite its initial successes, had ground to a halt. Enemy bombers and artillery had put roughly 20 of our tanks out of action, and our losses in terms of personnel rose to 500 men. The Panzer Lehr Division never fully recovered from this bloodshed.

This was typically how our attacks unfolded. It was a consequence not only of our shortage of artillery or ammunition but also our lack of air support that our initial penetration of the front was incapable of being expanded or developed into a breakthrough. The stubbornness and success of our resistance in the defence was second to none, but the prevailing combat conditions did not allow us to undertake anything more than local and limited counter-thrusts. Despite the outstanding tactical ability of our leadership and the untiring readiness of our men for action, the most that we could achieve in the end was to slow down the systematic forward movement of the enemy. This brought some degree of relief, which occasionally lasted several days.

In the middle of the month, the enemy attempted to execute a concentric offensive whose objective would be to bring about a decisive victory. Attacks were launched by both the British and American fronts. Both attacks ended with major German defensive successes.

Early in the morning on 18 July, the British VIII Corps, supported by the corps to either side, set off from Caen towards the plateau which lay beyond. This advance was preceded by extensive area bombing carried out by 2,100 aircraft belonging to the RAF, US Eighth Air Force, and US Ninth Air Force. The 21st Panzer Division and 16th Luftwaffe Field Division were hit hard. However, despite the damage done to our front-line positions by the enemy bombardment, we were still able to put up tough resistance further behind. Many of our 8.8cm anti-aircraft guns, so greatly feared by the enemy, had become available after the fall of Caen, and they now served effectively as a means of ground defence, destroying an extraordinarily large number of hostile combat vehicles. Several tactical successes ensued. There were already 175 burning or smouldering wrecks in the grainfields by the time the 1st SS Panzer Division Leibstandarte SS Adolf Hitler (SS-Major-General Theodor Wisch) destroyed another 75 tanks in a surprise attack launched at dawn and carried out throughout the morning. Such heavy losses were well beyond what the British had anticipated, and consequently Montgomery ended up making little progress. The attempt by the enemy to forcibly expand the beachhead between the Orne and the Dives had been thwarted. He managed to occupy neither Troarn nor the plateau southeast of Caen.

Unfortunately, on 17 July, the German leadership was dealt a devastating blow. Field Marshal Rommel was on his way to the front when, in the vicinity of Livarot (16 kilometres south of Lisieux), his vehicle was strafed by an enemy fighter-bomber. He was severely injured.

The major attack launched by the Americans unfolded in a manner similar to that by the British. Lying at the centre of the course of events was the Saint-Lô sector. The city was the capital of the department of Manche and was an important point through which traffic flowed. Nine roads, four of which were major highways, intersected here. The Vire flowed through the city along a deeply cut valley, which meant that the river bridge near Saint-Lô Station was of great strategic importance. It was there that the enemy would have the best opportunity to rapidly shift forces from one bank to the other. Despite our numerical inferiority, we possessed a defensive advantage in Saint-Lô. If the enemy wanted to neutralise this advantage, he would have no choice other than to force us out of the city.

Although the Americans had reached the valley of the Aire on 12 June, they had advanced no further for an entire month. Now, on 11 July, the US V Corps sought to advance on a wide front from the Forêt de Cerisy through Bérigny, which lay on the road connecting Saint-Lô and Bayeaux, with the intention of enveloping and then taking Saint-Lô from the east. A precondition for this action was the seizure of Hill 192. The struggle for control of this dominant hill was intense. A massive aerial bombardment conducted by the enemy was supposed to pave the way for an advance by ground forces against the II Parachute Corps (General of Parachute Troops Eugen Meindl), which was under the command of the LXXXIV Army Corps for the time being. Even though the hill itself was eventually lost, the fierce determination with which the road was held by two battalions belonging to the 3rd Parachute

Division (Lieutenant-General Richard Schimpf) – the III Battalion of the 9th Parachute Regiment and I Battalion of the 5th Parachute Regiment – meant that the enemy thrust could barely achieve a depth of 1.5 kilometres. Having suffered heavy casualties for little territorial gain, the enemy ground to a halt.

A second important combat sector lay near Carillon, approximately 5.5 kilometres north of Saint-Lô. We held a salient that jutted out between a couple of streams and encompassed a range of hills. While this position may have only been relatively lightly occupied by forces of the 266th and 352nd Infantry Divisions, it is a prime example of the effective overlapping of the arcs of fire of heavy machine guns, heavy mortars, and 8.8cm anti-aircraft guns. From 12–14 July, the US XIX Corps pushed against the Carillon salient. Its progress on the first day, despite the rolling barrage that supported it, amounted to only 200 metres. The enemy finally penetrated the front at Saint-Gilles, which was situated to the south of La Meauffe, and reached the main road that led to Saint-Lô at Pont-Hébert. With the enemy now deep in the rear of the Carillon salient, we were compelled, on 14 July, to evacuate what had until then been a thorn in the enemy's flesh. The ferocity of our resistance in every narrow gully, in every orchard, and in every village alleyway is highlighted by the remark of a soldier of the US 137th Infantry Regiment who had been taken prisoner: 'The Germans are fighting with extreme bitterness all along the front, literally obeying the order to die where they stand. Carillon is a stubbornly held German position.'

The Americans made a third attempt to break through to Saint-Lô on 18 July. By establishing firm contact with the British forces that stood to the south-east along the Caumont–Vidouville road, the Americans hoped to eliminate any danger of being outflanked by German forces. The Wehrmacht communiqué summarised the outcome of the fighting that day: 'The focal point lay in the area to the south-west of Balleroy, where American formations assembled and threatened to break through in the direction of Saint-Lô. They suffered heavy losses and were repelled. In this sector alone, more than 1,000 enemy troops were killed in action.' The performance of the German divisions in those days was amongst the most honourable of the entire war. With no reserves at their disposal whatsoever, they demonstrated dogged determination and tremendous fighting spirit.

Only gradually did the Americans draw closer to Saint-Lô, doing so from multiple directions. We had nothing more than half a company defending the north-western outskirts of the city! One of our bravest officers fell in close combat before the houses of those outskirts: Lieutenant-Colonel Hugo Freiherr von Aufseß, the commander of the 30th Mobile Brigade. He had only just reported that he had seen to it that the grave of General Marcks was in order. On the left bank of the Vire, the Panzer Lehr Division maintained its position at Hébécrevon, so it was from the east that the enemy infiltrated Saint-Lô. According to a report of ours that was written on 19 July at 1900 hours, the troops of the US 29th Infantry Division and US 113th Cavalry Group fought their way forward in small groups of five to 10 men, and under the protection of their tanks, into the ruins of the city. The German rearguard units withdrew step by step. Eventually, our artillery units withdrew as well. On 20 July, that very Thursday on which those fateful events unfolded in the Führer's headquarters in Germany[1] and the whole world sat up and took notice, the city that had been the location of the first headquarters of the LXXXIV Army Corps finally fell into the hands of the enemy. The last of the fighting in what had been the oldest and most beautiful parts of the city, especially in the medieval alleyways, came to an end. It had taken the enemy 44 days to reach Saint-Lô from his beachhead in Saint-Laurent and Colleville. He had originally envisioned that this distance would be covered in one week.

The weather deteriorated considerably. Continuous rain transformed the fields into mud and the roads into streams. Our tanks frequently got bogged down, and low cloud cover prevented enemy aerial activity. As a result, it became relatively quiet at the front. Both sides regrouped their forces. The fate that was in store for us was delayed by one week.

The ground forces of the Allies in Normandy on 20 July 1944 amounted to 30 infantry divisions and 13 armoured divisions. All were

---

1 Translator's note: Referred to here is the failed attempt by Colonel Claus von Stauffenberg to assassinate Hitler at the Wolf's Lair in East Prussia.

at full strength. There were in addition multiple special formations and reinforcement units with artillery, pioneer, and anti-tank troops. Opposing them on the German side were 20 infantry divisions and eight panzer divisions, although their combat strength varied dramatically. In the combat zone of the Seventh Army, the 91st Air Landing Division, consisting of only a few hundred men, stood at one end of the scale, while the 3rd Parachute Division, possessing more than 80 per cent of its original combat strength, was at the other. The average combat strength of the divisions of the Seventh Army was 40 per cent. Taking into consideration the availability of supplies and replacements on both sides, the ratio of Allied ground forces to German was three to one.

The collapse of the Cotentin front had come about more quickly than it should have due to an error on our part in regrouping our forces. On 25 July, the Seventh Army withdrew the 2nd Panzer Division from Caumont and allocated it to the XXXXVII Panzer Corps (General of Panzer Troops Hans Freiherr von Funck) so that, alongside the 116th Panzer Division, it could be committed to the sector south of Caen. It was there that Army Group B expected the next major enemy attack to take place. The 2nd Panzer Division was relieved without incident by the 326th Infantry Division (Lieutenant-General Viktor von Drabich-Wächter), which had until then been stationed in the Pas-de-Calais. However, the anticipated attack did not materialise. It took place instead the next day in the Saint-Lô sector, and the panzer formations were too far away to be able to intercept the American advance in time. We had taken a precautionary measure, but it had backfired. While the Allies could allow themselves the luxury of regularly taking precautionary measures, we could never afford to do so.

On 25 July, the US First Army commenced the major attack that would lead to the breakout from the beachhead. This attack grew in strength over the course of 26 and 27 July. The crisis that arose on the first day in the combat zone of the LXXXIV Army Corps was overcome by the 941st Grenadier Regiment (of the 353rd Infantry Division). The enemy had occupied the high ground to the south-east of Lozon, but the grenadier regiment retook this high ground and absorbed what few elements remained of the 5th Parachute Division (Lieutenant-General Gustav Wilke).

On 27 July, 1,500 heavy bombers tore open the German front to the north of the road connecting Saint-Lô, Périers, and Lessay. They concentrated their efforts on an area 5 kilometres in width and 2.5 kilometres in depth. At precisely 1100 hours, the infantry and armoured forces of multiple American divisions set off on a narrow front. They were protected nonstop by 400 fighter-bombers, the enemy aircraft pouncing on any machine-gun or artillery positions that opened fire.

The enemy gained up to 3.5 kilometres of ground, although the German right flank held its position. The army corps had moved the 353rd Infantry Division there from its northern front, and the Americans were now brought to a halt on that flank.

The II Parachute Corps was involved in heavy fighting on those three days. Its left boundary was subjected to carpet bombing, and the extensive activity of low-flying aircraft in the rear area revealed that the Americans wanted to establish complete control over the road junction in Saint-Lô so that they could pivot to the east and strike the flank of the parachute corps. General Meindl committed the last of his reserves, the 15th Parachute Regiment, to the battle. To the south of the bend in the Vire, the boundary between the inner wings of the parachute corps and the army corps was prised open, thereby exposing the flanks of these formations. A gap developed to the south-east of Marigny that was unable to be closed. The result was a breakthrough for the enemy in the middle of the combat zone of the Seventh Army.

The front line of the parachute corps on the morning of 27 July formed a large northward-facing curve whose course ran as follows: La Lande (south-east of Caumont)–Vidouville–Bérigny–southern side of the N177 highway to La Barre–Fuchiron–south-west bank of the Vire–Gourfaleur. From his position in the vicinity of Canisy, the enemy would have the choice of wheeling to the east or west. Either way, he would be able to bring about the collapse of the entire front of the Seventh Army. There were no more reserves at our disposal. The 12th Parachute Reconnaissance Battalion took up a position of all-round defence at the road junction in Le Mesnil-Herman and served there as a wave-breaker. It disabled

84 • NORMANDY

Map 10: The withdrawal of the LXXXIV Army Corps to the south-east

eight American tanks and held the enemy back long enough so that the headquarters of the 352nd Infantry Division would have time to evacuate the forest that lay to the north-west of the road junction. The forces of the infantry division that were still located to the west of the Vire were intercepted by the leading tanks of the approaching US 2nd Armored Division. The army corps scraped together two panzer and two infantry companies in order to cover the gap on its right flank.

There was only one possible course of action in this situation, and that was to withdraw with the idea of shortening the front line and freeing up forces for the interception of any further enemy attacks. This withdrawal was carried out on 28 July.

The forces of the LXXXIV Army Corps held what was called the Blue Line for just one day on 26 July. On the right wing, near Canisy, was the Panzer Lehr Division, and it sought with great effort, in conjunction with elements of the 275th Infantry Division, to set up an obstacle line that would seal the open flank of the army corps. American tanks swarmed through the gap in the front and drove as far as Hambye, after which they suddenly circled to the south-west.

This line of advance clearly showed that the enemy objective was to reach the coast either at Coutances or Avranches. The manoeuvre that had been carried out at Saint-Sauveur-le-Vicomte on 18 June would now be repeated on a larger scale and could very well lead to the army corps being cut off. The Seventh Army therefore ordered that a withdrawal to the south-east be conducted without regard for any contact that might be made with the enemy. Only a few rearguard units would be left behind to tie down enemy forces that attempted to apply direct pressure in pursuit.

General von Choltitz vehemently opposed the plan to withdraw from what was referred to as the Red Line (Hambye–Roncey–Coutances–mouth of the Sienne) towards the south-east. He insisted that a withdrawal from the west coast would create a gap through which the US VIII Corps could advance to the south. On top of that, such a withdrawal would have to be conducted through terrain controlled by the US VII Corps and would therefore be slow and costly. He knew, of course, that an eventual breakthrough by the enemy could not be prevented, but it could at least be delayed. Only once the enemy reached Avranches would the breakthrough become a reality. The coast bent sharply to the west there, meaning that the security of our left flank would be unable to be guaranteed from then on. Any time that could be gained, even if only a few days, would be of the utmost importance for counter-measures in the rear area of the current position. On the evening of 28 July, Field Marshal Günther von Kluge, the commander of OB West, countermanded the order of the Seventh Army to withdraw to the south-east and ordered instead that a withdrawal be conducted to the south. However, this order did not reach the headquarters of the army corps until 2200 hours, by which time the movement to the south-east was already underway. Any attempt at that time to halt this movement would have caused utter confusion within the chain of command of the army corps. The costly march therefore ran its course.

Two engagements that took place on the night of 28/29 July are worthy of mention. The 2nd Panzer Division had just arrived on the right wing, and its 304th Panzer Grenadier Regiment took the road junction in La Denisière, thereby cutting through the road connecting Saint-Lô and Percy. The enemy suffered heavy casualties and lost 30 of his tanks. A battle group of the panzer division established a defensive position and remained there like a thorn in the enemy's side until 30 July. After that, seven tanks of the battle group fought their way back to the main body of the panzer division.

In the combat zone of the 353rd Infantry Division, the 941st Grenadier Regiment breached the enemy front at Saint-Denis-le-Gast, and it was through there that our forces were able to escape. The crossings over the Sienne were not blocked, and this allowed the infantry division to reach the opposite bank of the river with relatively few losses. This was done overnight and completed by the afternoon of 29 July. With the remains of the 243rd Infantry Division and those of Battle Group Heinz (of the 275th Infantry Division) placed under its command, the total strength of the 353rd Infantry Division amounted to only 400 men.

The days around 28 July were like a surreal nightmare. Waves of American tanks, protected by waves of low-flying aircraft, flowed through the gap in the front towards the south. Our units lost contact with one another. Smaller groups, cut off or under pressure, probed weak points of the enemy lines and bypassed localities where enemy resistance was strong. Once our forces reassembled, they drove back the enemy armoured spearheads and prevented the complete collapse of our front. The fighting dissolved into smaller skirmishes, especially on hills and at road junctions. Our non-commissioned officers demonstrated the utmost independence and initiative. They and the men under their command clung to tactically important landmarks, never panicking despite the chaotic conditions around them.

The telephone lines were lost as a means by which the army corps could communicate orders. Although the men of the corps signal battalion worked until they dropped, they did not have time to remove our telephone lines while the withdrawal was being conducted. These lines simply remained where they were, extending across many kilometres of terrain, and the result was that the army corps could no longer control the formations on its flanks.

Communications now had to be transmitted by radio or via orderly officers. These young lieutenants had to ride their motorcycles behind an ever-changing front line and beneath constantly buzzing fighter-bombers. That they managed to accomplish their tasks is a demonstration of their determination, vigilance, and composure. Even the chief of staff of the army corps succeeded, during the night, in making his way through to the battle group of the 243rd Infantry Division at Hyenville and then to the remaining forces of the 2nd SS Panzer Division Das Reich at Trelly. It would have otherwise been impossible to obtain a clear picture of the situation, and all we would have had to go by were the contradictory rumours about the presence of enemy tanks.

The headquarters of the LXXXIV Army Corps was at that time in Le Mesnil-Aubert, which lay to the north-east of Cérences. Several low-flying aircraft struck the hamlet in the afternoon: any activity at the command post was neutralised for a long time. Towards the evening, motor noises could be clearly heard on the road, just 1 kilometre away, that led to Cérences. American tanks were advancing through Lengronne and coming to a halt on the outskirts of Cérences. General von Choltitz was able to follow their movements from his window thanks to the trails of smoke that rose in the air and the explosions of gunfire that drew ever nearer. It seemed as if the route of retreat of the army corps had been cut off.

Our visual observations then suggested that the enemy spearheads had started to move back. The outer districts of Cérences seemed to be free of enemy forces. This gave us the opportunity, shortly before midnight, to commence the shift of the headquarters of the army corps to Le Tann-sur-Airou, which was situated to the south of Gavray. The view that greeted us on the way was greatly distressing. A long column had been destroyed and was strewn along the road. Dead horses, smouldering wood, and red-hot iron lay everywhere. Flames emanating from Cérences lit up the surroundings so that it was as bright as day. Any movement could have been spotted by enemy aircraft. Ever so gradually, step by step, we made our way forward. Rubble had to be cleared from our path every 20 metres, and further pauses were necessary during periods of enemy aerial activity.

At the height of this crisis, the headquarters of the army corps was dealt another blow, with General von Choltitz being relieved and replaced with Lieutenant-General Otto Elfeldt. At the same time, Major-General Max Pemsel, the chief of staff of the Seventh Army, had to step aside for Colonel Rudolf-Christoph Freiherr von Gersdorff. Scapegoats were being found for the looming breakthrough of the Americans!

The Seventh Army, the command post of which was in Chavoy (near Avranches), made use of all the means at its disposal to prepare for what was to come. The remains of decimated divisions were placed under the command of other divisions, while the headquarters staff thereby made available were employed to seal off roads leading south and to organise stragglers into standby units. To ensure that these new units received rations and equipment, some of the personnel of existing supply units had to be handed over to them. There was much improvisation, but it was generally of little use. The downcast troops lacked armour-piercing weaponry and were organised in a makeshift manner. Assigned to unfamiliar units and commanded by unfamiliar officers, they had no time to develop a new sense of a common fighting spirit.

Choltitz had wanted to retreat to the Green Line on 26 July, but it was only reached on 29 July. This line ran as follows: Percy–Sourdeval–south

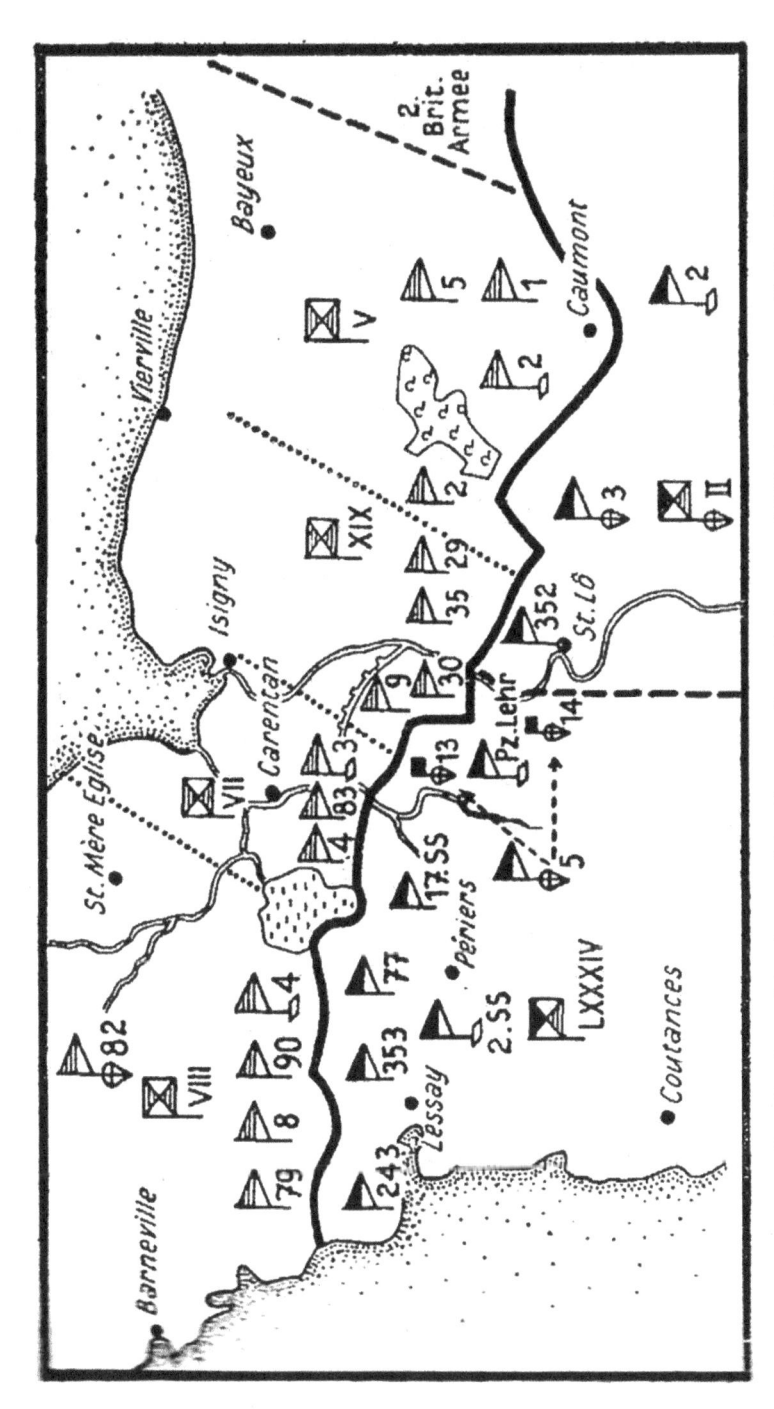

THE BREAKTHROUGH OF THE AMERICANS (26 JUNE–31 JULY 1944) • 89

Map 11: Distribution of the forces of the German Seventh Army and US First Army on 11 July 1944

bank of the Sienne–Cérences–Bréhal. Percy would later become the fulcrum of the new front of the Seventh Army.

As early as 30 July, the US 4th Armored Division, after 20,000 rounds of preparatory fire had been laid down, overran the paper-thin Green Line. The only roadblock was formed by the forwardmost battery of an assault gun battalion that had just arrived from Rennes. The 353rd Infantry Division set off on the night of 30/31 July for Villedieu and, with its meagre 800 men, set up a new line of resistance on either side of the town. The defence of the town itself was entrusted to the 957th Grenadier Regiment (Colonel Waldemar Freiherr von Gall), which belonged to the 363rd Infantry Division. To the left, on either side of L'Épine, stood the 116th Panzer Division. A new front was in the process of being formed, but the forces assigned to hold it, now so far from the coast, could do nothing for the time being other than to observe the enemy.

The breakthrough becomes reality!

If one statement can be made about the rush of events from 25–30 July, it is that the attrition of our forces in Normandy had reached a level that threatened to bring about the collapse of the weakly defended front.

A comparison of German and American forces at the time of the departure of Choltitz from the army corps is worthwhile at this point. Under the command of the army corps were battle groups created from what was left of three infantry formations (the 91st Air Landing Division, 243rd Infantry Division, and 353rd Infantry Division), two panzer formations (the 2nd SS Panzer Division Das Reich and Panzer Lehr Division), one panzer grenadier formation (the 17th SS Panzer Grenadier Division Götz von Berlichingen), and one parachute formation (the 5th Parachute Division). On 10 July, the combat strength of the 353rd Infantry Division amounted to 1,500 men and that of the 243rd Infantry Division 700 men. These numbers were of course much lower by the end of July. By then, the 243rd Infantry Division and Battle Group Heinz each comprised just 200 men. Neither formation possessed artillery. The 6th Parachute Regiment, which had been engaged in combat ever since the battle of Carentan, consisted of only 40 men. This meant that the real strength of the army corps at the end of July equated to approximately one full-strength infantry division and one half-strength panzer division.

We did not have a clear picture of the order of battle of the Americans, mainly because they had reorganised their forces, but we were at least aware of the presence of the US VII Corps (with the 4th, 9th, and 83rd Infantry Divisions and the 4th Armored Division) and the US VIII Corps (with the 8th, 79th, and 90th Infantry Divisions and the 3rd Armored Division). Also identified were units of the 6th Armored Division. Given the constant arrival of fresh men and equipment, we could assume that most of the enemy formations were at full strength.

In addition to his numerical superiority, the enemy enjoyed several other advantages. First, his forces were fully motorised, which gave him good mobility and ensured the protection of his infantry. Second, according to his wartime table of organisation, the enemy equipped his artillery regiments such that they were stronger than ours by 30 per cent, while his armoured battalions were each allocated 51 vehicles. Third, his supply of fuel and ammunition, as well as that of his first-rate rations, was practically unlimited. Fourth, his certainty of final victory gave him a tremendous psychological boost. Fifth, his aircraft dominated the skies. There can be no surprise, considering all these factors, that the enemy breakthrough succeeded. What is surprising is that we managed to delay this breakthrough until 30 July.

It is illuminating to examine the Allied operational plan and to compare the dates on which certain objectives were intended to be reached with those on which they were actually reached. The table below presents this information in terms of the number of days after D-Day. It shows that the Allies made much slower progress than they had hoped for and explains why they committed more divisions to combat than they had originally intended.

Objective	Reached on	Planned	Actual
Caen	9 July 1944	D+1	D+33
Cherbourg	29 June 1944	D+6	D+19
Saint-Lô	20 July 1944	D+8	D+44
Avranches	1 August 1944	D+20	D+54

In the Fatherland, on 1 August, the Wehrmacht communiqué reported on the breakout of the Americans from the narrow beachhead as follows: 'The enemy forces that penetrated deep into our position on the west wing were intercepted by a counter-thrust immediately to the south of Avranches. During the night, heavy bombers caried out effective raids against enemy concentrations of troops and areas of assembly to the north-west of Avranches.'

The Allies were ready to advance far into the north-western part of France. The period of mobile warfare had begun.

CHAPTER 4

The Falaise pocket

The Wehrmacht communiqué of 1 August 1944 revealed to the German public that the fighting in France was no longer limited to the Cotentin Peninsula. The enemy thrusts towards Brittany, the Seine, and the Loire were a clear indication that the coastal battle was developing into a war of movement that would spread across the north-west of France.

The changing situation prompted both sides to reorganise their forces. The US Twelfth Army Group came into being under the command of Lieutenant General Omar Bradley. At the disposal of this formation were the old US First Army (Lieutenant General Courtney Hodges with the V, VII, and XIX Corps) and the recently arrived US Third Army (Lieutenant General George S. Patton with the VIII, XII, XV, and XX Corps). While the forces under Hodges would push straight to the east in the direction of Vire and Mortain, those under Patton would form the envelopment wing of the enemy front by fanning out to the west, south, and south-east. On 10 August, the US Third Army temporarily handed over the XV Corps, which had departed a little further to the left at Le Mans, to the US First Army. British forces were concentrated under the 21st Army Group of General Bernard Montgomery. This formation consisted of the old Second Army (Lieutenant-General Miles Dempsey) and, newly operational on 23 July, the Canadian First Army (Lieutenant-General Harry Crerar). While Crerar would advance between the Orne and the Dives along the Caen–Falaise road towards the south, Dempsey would assume responsibility for the right wing of the British sector of the front.

The reorganisation of our forces at that time proved to be the prelude to a series of frequent changes in command at the highest levels of the German Army in the West. The Caen sector was held by the Fifth Panzer Army, which had previously been Panzer Group West. Its commander, General of Panzer Troops Leo Geyr von Schweppenburg, had already been replaced on 5 July by General of Panzer Troops Heinrich Eberbach. When the situation at Mortain reached a deadlock, the OKW transferred the most effective combat formation of the Fifth Panzer Army – Panzer Group Eberbach – to the southern front. It was hoped that Eberbach's thorough knowledge of and extensive experience in the employment of panzer forces would help to restore the situation. Command of the Fifth Panzer Army itself, which remained in the vicinity of Caen with battered units, passed to SS-General Sepp Dietrich, formerly the commander of the I SS Panzer Corps.

To the left of the Fifth Panzer Army was the Seventh Army, at the disposal of which was the II Parachute Corps and LXXXIV Army Corps. The former was commanded by General of Parachute Troops Eugen Meindl and was responsible for the sector stretching from the boundary with the Fifth Panzer Army to the area near Vire. The latter had been under the command of Lieutenant-General Otto Elfeldt since 29 July, and most of the old divisional numbers had disappeared from its maps. All that remained was a battle group of the 353rd Infantry Division. The front line of the army corps on 7 August ran as follows: Vire–southern edge of the Forêt de Saint-Sever near Champ-du-Boult–Calvados–Saint-Pois–valley of the Sée near Le Mesnil-Gilbert.

Operation *Lüttich* was the name of the counter-thrust that was to be carried out westwards from Mortain through lost territory towards the west coast, and its execution required the creation of a special panzer group. Under the overall command of the XXXXVII Panzer Corps (General of Panzer Troops Hans Freiherr von Funck), this panzer group consisted of six panzer divisions. From the XXXXVII Panzer Corps itself were the 2nd Panzer Division (Lieutenant-General Heinrich Freiherr von Lüttwitz) and 116th Panzer Division (Lieutenant-General Gerhard Graf von Schwerin), from the I SS Panzer Corps (SS-General Georg Keppler) were battalions from the 1st SS Panzer Division Leibstandarte SS Adolf Hitler (SS-Major-General Theodor Wisch) and 2nd SS Panzer Division Das Reich (SS-Colonel Otto Baum), and from the II SS Panzer

Corps (SS-General Wilhelm Bittrich) were the 9th SS Panzer Division Hohenstaufen (SS-Colonel Sylvester Stadler) and 10th SS Panzer Division Frundsberg (SS-Colonel Heinz Harmel). It ought to be mentioned that these panzer forces could never be properly assembled. The pressure applied by the enemy on the ground and in the air allowed barely any time for such assembly if we wanted to launch an attack. On top of that, both formations on the flanks ended up being largely absent from the thrust at Mortain, for the 116th Panzer Division had to deal with a number of crises in the combat zone of the LXXXIV Army Corps and the 9th SS Panzer Division Hohenstaufen had to do the same in the combat zone, on the southern front, of the LXXXI Army Corps.

It was the LXXXI Army Corps, initially headquartered at Rouen and commanded by General of Cavalry Adolf-Friedrich Kuntzen, that took over responsibility for the left flank of the German front in Normandy on 1 August. The forces to the south of Domfront came under the command of this army corps, but those forces were rather weak. Elements of the 708th Infantry Division had arrived from Royan, which lay at the mouth of the Garonne, while some of the forces of the 9th Panzer Division had rolled forward from southern France. There were also the forces that belonged to the 1st Motorised Security Regiment. The primary task of the army corps was to monitor the enemy at the most crucial point of the Mortain front; otherwise, the line it held was as follows: Barenton – Domfront – east bank of the Varenne – east bank of the Mayenne. Between the boundary of the LXXXI Army Corps and the Loire were only a couple of formations belonging to the LXXX Army Corps, headquartered in Poitiers. Those formations were Blocking Force Kortüm (later Blocking Force Heckel) and the 158th Infantry Division (headquartered in Fontenay-le-Comte), and it would be their task to block the progress of the US Third Army. Along the Mayenne, between Laval in the north and Angers in the south, were a small number of naval standby units.

What follows is a summary of the most important events that took place during the fighting from 1–20 August:

31 July–15 August
Battle of Saint-Malo.

6 August
Capture of Mont Pinçon by the British 43rd (Wessex) Infantry Division.

7–8 August
Counter-attack of the XXXXVII Panzer Corps at Mortain towards the west.

7–9 August
First attack of the Canadian First Army, which proceeded along the Caen–Falaise road with the intention of enabling an advance along the valley of the Orne.

9–10 August
Crisis at La-Lande-Vaumont, in the combat zone of the LXXXIV Army Corps, brought about by a flank attack launched by the Americans from the north-west.

10 August
Departure, on our left, of the US XV Corps from Le Mans for the purpose of encircling our Seventh Army.

11 August
Shortening of our front line in the vicinity of Mortain.

13–14 August
Panzer Group Eberbach engaged in combat near Alençon, on our southern flank.

14–17 August
Second Canadian attack conducted from the Laison River towards Falaise.

17 August
Advance by the British towards Condé and Tinchebray. Infiltration by the US V Corps of the southern part of Argentan. Field Marshal Günther von Kluge replaced by Field Marshal Walter Model as commander of OB West.

THE FALAISE POCKET · 97

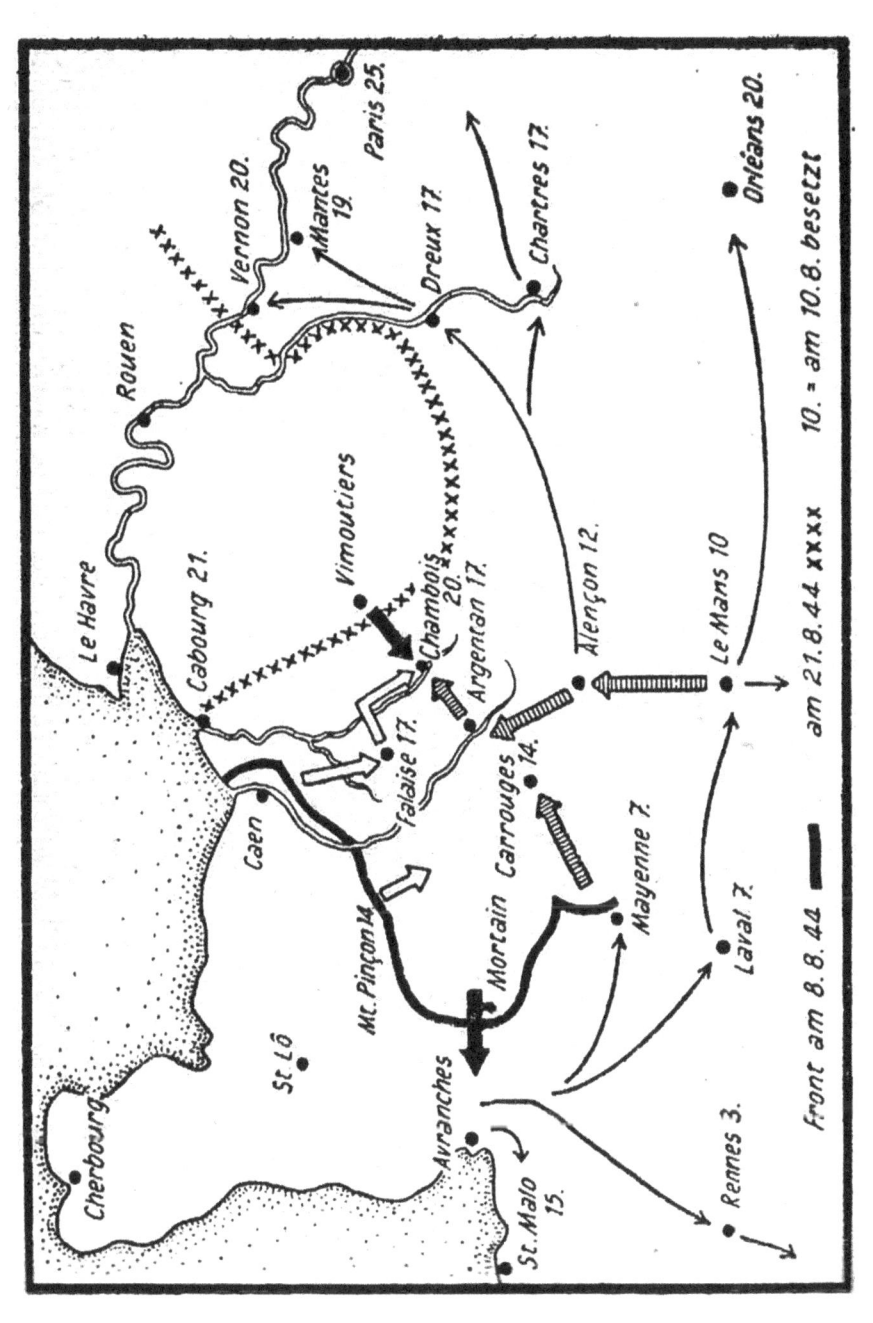

Map 12: The Falaise pocket

19 August
Battle of Chambois.

20 August
Counter-thrust of the II SS Panzer Corps from Vimoutiers towards Trun and Saint-Lambert to the south-west. Breakouts conducted by various German battle groups.

Our supply was in a state of chaos. After the breakthrough at Avranches, the Seventh Army, at first partly and then entirely, had to be supplied by the Fifth Panzer Army. This overtaxed our already poorly functioning supply columns. It frequently became the case that one night was not enough time to complete any one delivery. The situation was constantly changing, and our column commanders could not always be kept informed. As a result, they sometimes ended up wandering around for hours in the rear area. The condition of the roads and the presence of fighter-bombers only made their work more difficult. Despite the outstanding efforts of the chief quartermaster of OB West, Colonel Eberhard Finckh, a shortage of fuel and ammunition could not be avoided. When this indispensable officer was brought before the People's Court in Berlin as someone who had been in the know about the assassination attempt against Hitler, our supply organisation rapidly slid into decay. This was especially disadvantageous for us on our left flank, where the Americans were advancing from Le Mans towards Alençon. In the months before the invasion of Normandy had begun, it was in the vicinity of Alençon that many of the supply depots of the Seventh Army had been placed. Although they were camouflaged in extensive forests, the opportunity to make them mobile had been missed. Large quantities of supplies, unable to be moved, had to be destroyed or allowed to fall into the hands of the enemy. There were some locations where the French population raided depots for rations.

Our signal communications failed more and more often. Most of our telephone lines in the rear area led through Le Mans and Alençon. Once both those towns had fallen, there were very few lines that remained at our disposal, and they became greatly overburdened with communications traffic. Low-flying aircraft and technical problems rendered many of our radio stations ineffective.

The Seventh Army had only the refreshed and refitted 77th Infantry Division (Colonel Rudolf Bacherer) with which to resist the breakthrough of the Americans on 31 July. This infantry division ended up being engaged in the fighting at Saint-Malo. It had been detached from the LXXXIV Army Corps on 17 July so that it could be brought to full strength in the vicinity of Dinant as quickly as possible. The combat elements of the infantry division had returned to the front before its headquarters could do so, for General von Choltitz needed every man he could get. Those combat units were augmented not only by the replacements they had received but also by the elements of other divisions that had belonged to the army corps and were at that time struggling along the west coast within visual range of Mont Saint-Michel. On 30 July, Colonel Bacherer received the following radio message from OB West: 'Avranches is to be occupied and held at all costs. It is the key element of our defence. The outcome of the war in the West will depend on whether the town stands or falls.'

The counter-thrust of the infantry division commenced on the afternoon of 31 July. Support was provided by an assault gun brigade that had just arrived at the front, and although the infantry division managed to reach its objective, it was forced back shortly thereafter due to the pressure applied by the US 4th and 8th Armored Divisions.

In accordance with the orders he had been given, Colonel Bacherer conducted delaying action so as to allow time for the organisation of our defences in Saint-Malo. On the morning of 1 August, the American armoured battalions on the Pontaubault–Pontorson road suffered heavy losses, with 34 of their tanks being put out of action by our flak units. The enemy advance slowed considerably. In Dol, the American officer in charge of the repair of damaged harbours was killed when he drove his armoured car into an area held by German security units. Found in his bag were papers with details on the extent of the damage that had been done to the harbour installations in Saint-Malo. The city commandant was Colonel Andreas von Aulock, and he decided that the 77th Infantry Division would be placed to the west of the Rance

River while the 46th Patrol Boat Flotilla would serve as a floating battery on that river.

The final battle for the citadel, which stood by the sea on Hill 26, commenced one week later. The primary purpose of this fortification was the prevention of enemy seaborne landings, but it also possessed interconnected blockhouses that faced inland. It was stocked with food and water, and the Luftwaffe had promised to deliver further supplies. However, despite two attempts by the Luftwaffe to keep its promise, barely any of those supplies were delivered. Mist concealed the drop point during the first attempt, and only two aircraft made it through the enemy anti-aircraft defences during the second. In the fortification were approximately 700 men, a number that greatly exceeded operational needs and available supplies. Colonel Bacherer therefore ordered that those of his men who were fathers of multiple children were to surrender themselves to the Americans, and he decided that members of supply units were to do the same. This took place on 14 August, prior to the commencement of the enemy attack, although the US 83rd Infantry Division, provided with covering fire, had in the meantime pushed forward gradually and had infiltrated our outer lines. Early on 15 August, from a conquered strongpoint whose telephone line to the German divisional headquarters remained intact, the American commander, Major General Robert C. Macon, demanded of the German commandant that he capitulate. This was rejected, although a temporary truce was agreed so that the wounded in the citadel could be handed over to the enemy and provided with immediate care.

The Americans opened fire on the hill at 1400 hours, making use of high-explosive shells and white phosphorus hand grenades. A lucky hit set stored ammunition on fire and led to the explosion of further stocks. The fumes penetrated the casemates. Since there was no ventilation system, the garrison was in danger of death by suffocation. Phosphorous smoke caused the straw beds to catch fire. Tunnels collapsed as shells exploded, burying many of the defenders. With ever more smoke, it became increasingly apparent that there was no escape, and it was for that reason that the white flag was raised above the citadel. Some 350 survivors were taken prisoner. So chivalrous was the American commander that he allowed Colonel Bacherer a parting word to his men.

On the main front, the rest of the LXXXIV Army Corps withdrew to the south-east on 31 July. Enemy tanks repeatedly plunged into the withdrawing army corps from the north, isolating and sometimes destroying smaller groups. An example of this can be seen when the command post of the army corps was shifted from Le Tann to Brécy between the late hours of 31 July and the early hours of 1 August. As always, it was carried out in a manner such that the corps command echelon remained in the old location until the corps intelligence section, which had gone on ahead, reached the new one. However, on this occasion, the corps intelligence section waited in vain for the remaining elements of the headquarters of the army corps. Enemy aerial activity had been preventing any movement since 0830 hours. Not only the fleet of headquarters vehicles but also two companies of the corps signal battalion, a further 100 vehicles, two horse-drawn batteries, and approximately 200 stragglers from various divisions found makeshift cover on secondary roads and in orchards. No consideration could be given to moving further forward until nightfall. It was soon reported that enemy tanks had already appeared further to the east and that the head of the corps map section had been shot while he had been laying out maps ready for distribution.

The day went by very slowly. At 1700 hours, the noise of tracked vehicles could be heard close by. The third general staff officer of the army corps concealed himself behind some sheaves of wheat on high ground and counted the American tanks that rolled by on the country road. They were barely 250 metres away. An entire armoured battalion pushed forward between our observers and what was presumably our front line. It seemed as if the enemy spearhead had reached its objective for the day, for it came to a halt on the outskirts of Brécy and took up a position of all-round defence on the other side of the destroyed bridge. The wind carried laughs and snippets of conversation between French women and American soldiers. We eagerly awaited nightfall and remained unseen thanks to the fact that the enemy security units stayed close to their tanks.

At dusk, the third general staff officer set off by bicycle to issue instructions for the planned breakout. None of the reconnaissance units that had been sent to find a suitable route of retreat had returned, so the third general staff officer, accompanied by two other officers from the corps intelligence section, went in search of a point at which the enemy-controlled road could best be crossed. When they were a short distance from where the secondary road entered the Villedieu–Brécy country road, a sudden concentration of fire nearby lit up the terrain and compelled them to take cover in the roadside ditch. The enemy sentries were so close that the glowing ends of their cigarettes could be clearly seen, and it was only there, at the point where most of the American troops had stopped, that there existed the best prospects of evading the enemy tanks that had been detected.

The retreat across the road commenced at midnight. After some short bursts of fire, the enemy sentries withdrew. A Sherman tank that controlled the stretch of road where we crossed was knocked out with rocket-propelled grenades. This stretch was temporarily secured with two artillery pieces, and our troops, who had been cut off until then, set off as quickly as possible in the direction of Saint-Pois. They reached the German lines an hour later. This experience was only one of very many from the war and may even be regarded as somewhat trivial, yet it meant a great deal for those who participated in it.

The panzer counter-attack at Mortain

In the first week of August, the leadership of the German Army in the West assembled strong panzer forces in the vicinity of Mortain. The objective would be an operational counter-thrust in the direction of the west coast at Avranches. If the advance of the enemy forces in France was to be checked at all, this was the only course of action to pursue. An immediate withdrawal to the Seine could not be considered, for this would have meant the abandonment of southern France and of the German troops stationed there under the command of Army Group Blaskowitz, or more specifically the Nineteenth Army (headquartered in Avignon). A significant amount of materiel would have been lost as well.

This attempt to close the gap that was coming into being would have to be carried out before the gradually advancing enemy had pushed forward too far. Field Marshal von Kluge had already decided during a visit to the command post of the Seventh Army in Mortain on 31 July that such an operation would be necessary. The headquarters of the Seventh Army had made it clear that the conduct of this operation would be dependent not only on the development of the situation on the southern front but also on the time of the arrival of reinforcements. While the assembly of the forces of the XXXXVII Panzer Corps was underway, an exhaustively detailed plan for the attack arrived from the Führer's headquarters. It was delivered by General of Artillery Walter Warlimont.

According to this plan, the supply lines of the US Third Army, which was conducting operations in the north-west of France, were to be cut off, while the remaining enemy forces in the beachhead were to be contained. It would then be possible to decisively delay and disrupt the strategic plans of the Allies. Hitler's far-reaching expectations were recorded in the war diary of OB West: 'After the successful penetration of the enemy front, the attacking formations are to pivot to the north and thrust deep into the flank and rear of the hostile forces before the Seventh Army with the objective of bringing about the collapse of the entire enemy front in Normandy.'

In theory, the plan was simple and brilliant. However, the assembly of our tanks took a whole week. Every day that passed by worked to our disadvantage, which meant that it would be incorrect to adhere strictly to the original plan. In fact, even the opportunity for a limited success had been missed. This was drily expressed by Kluge, shortly before he committed suicide, in a letter to Hitler: 'Your order was based on conditions that did not at all exist. When I read this decisive order, I immediately gained the impression that what was being demanded here was something that would go down in history as a tremendously bold operation but that, unfortunately, would be impossible to carry out in practice.'

It was at about that time that the third general staff officer of the LXXXIV Army Corps rescued a volume of the memoirs of Marshal

Auguste de Marmont from the ruins of a palace in Saint-Jean-des-Bois, south of Tinchebray. While leafing through the book, he came across a passage whose assessment, though it referred to the completely inappropriate orders that had been issued by Napoleon I for the conduct of the withdrawal fighting in Spain in the spring of 1811, seemed to apply perfectly for Hitler's overly ambitious plan: 'The emperor was living in a world that existed not in actuality but only in his own imagination. He made things up out of thin air, mistaking wishes for realities and giving orders as if he knew nothing of the true situation or as if facts were deliberately being concealed from him!' It would hardly be possible to find a better way to describe the inflexibility with which the decision was made to go ahead with the operation at Mortain.

Objections to the plan were raised not only by the headquarters of the Seventh Army but also by that of the Fifth Panzer Army. The assembly of strong panzer forces at Mortain meant the weakening of our front against the British near Caen. Despite this, Hitler wanted the operation to go ahead and issued a directive to that effect. To not follow this directive would have amounted to insubordination, so Kluge toed the line despite his better judgement.

There was also concern at the headquarters of the LXXXIV Army Corps. The formation had been reduced in strength, and it had lost its earlier status as an army detachment. Covering the right flank of the panzer thrust, it soon felt the effects of the counteraction of the US First Army. Even so, the army corps was allocated the 363rd Infantry Division (Major-General August Dettling) and 84th Infantry Division (Major-General Erwin Menny). The former assumed responsibility for the right wing of the army corps in the vicinity of Vire, where it faced the British, while the latter, which had just been constituted near Rouen, failed to meet expectations. Most of its personnel lacked combat experience, and even its subordinate leadership was not fully capable. The 84th Infantry Division was therefore of little value when committed to the front. It was an enormous risk to have to employ this formation in a sector which had previously only been held with the greatest possible effort by panzer forces.

THE FALAISE POCKET • 105

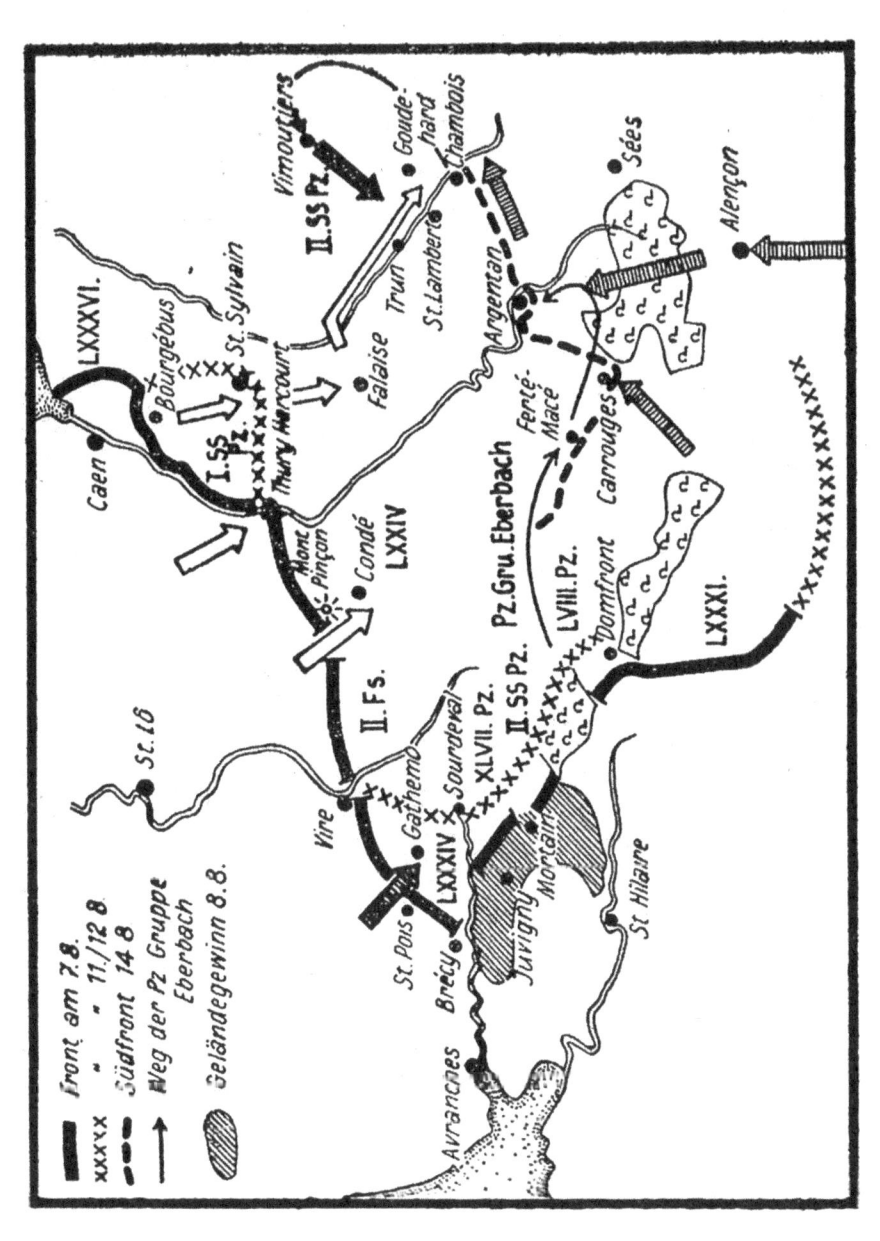

Map 13: German panzer forces, 7–20 August 1944

The remains of the tried and tested 352nd Infantry Division were detached from the II Parachute Corps. The commander of the infantry division, Lieutenant-General Dietrich Kraiß, died in a field hospital on the night of 2 August, having been severely wounded in an air strike carried out by enemy fighter-bombers. The detached elements were assembled as a battle group in the vicinity of Alençon. Under the command of Major-General Eberhard von Schluckmann, the battle group was subsequently positioned to the north-west of Paris.

The concentration of panzer forces by the Seventh Army was largely complete by 5 August. There were 120 German tanks ready to advance in the direction of Avranches. They would make use of the terrain between the Sée and the Sélune, the valleys of which were natural obstacles providing good flank protection against enemy tanks. The roads led from east to west and were therefore favourable for the conduct of our attack and the flow of our supplies. Observation to the north and south would be possible thanks to the high ground between the valleys.

The XXXXVII Panzer Corps set off on the night of 6/7 August. While the 2nd Panzer Division made good progress, the left wing was delayed due to difficulties encountered by the 1st SS Panzer Division Leibstandarte SS Adolf Hitler. The commander of the panzer regiment of this SS formation had neglected to scout out multiple routes of advance, and the result was that his troops got stuck in a narrow valley 2 kilometres in length. A British fighter-bomber that had been shot down plunged into the leading tanks, causing the entire SS panzer regiment to grind to a halt. Our vehicles had to retrace their steps, meaning that the attack was delayed by hours and only made a proper start in broad daylight. The formations that partook in the thrust, from north to south, were the 116th Panzer Division (north of the valley of the Sée), 2nd Panzer Division (reinforced with elements of the 1st SS Panzer Division Leibstandarte SS Adolf Hitler), and 2nd SS Panzer Division Das Reich (on either side of Mortain). Echeloned to the rear were a small battle group of the 17th SS Panzer Grenadier Division Götz von Berlichingen and another small battle group of the Panzer Lehr Division. The tanks belonging to the army were tremendously successful. Although the main reason for the enemy's progress thus far had been his dominance of the skies, early morning mist on this day initially kept his aircraft on the ground. The German spearhead overran the American lines and advanced 8 kilometres whilst suffering barely any casualties. The 2nd SS Panzer Division Das Reich seized Mortain and pushed further in the direction of Saint-Hilaire. Despite this success, the mopping-up operations in the areas that had been taken lasted for some time. The encircled I Battalion of the US 177th Infantry Regiment was supplied from the air and fought especially hard, receiving the honorary title 'the 30th's famed lost battalion'.

What could not be achieved by American ground forces was so by the RAF Second Tactical Air Force once the weather cleared. Lieutenant-General Alfred Bülowius, the commander of the II Fighter Corps, had promised full air support, assuring the chief of staff of the Seventh Army: 'Three hundred fighters will sweep back and forth across the skies and over the ridges of land early on 7 August.' The German Army made it clear that such fighter cover would be absolutely necessary if the attack were to have any chance of success. However, not a single machine appeared over the battlefield! The fighter formations had probably taken off, only to become involved in heavy combat above their home fields around Paris. This left our tanks vulnerable, and they were hit hard, with rocket-firing Typhoons inflicting the heaviest casualties. This day, 7 August 1944, was the first time in the history of warfare that a strong ground attack was entirely stopped from the air. Road mines that had been laid by the enemy were just one further hindrance. It had not been possible to reach Avranches in a single stroke. Even so, the situation was not completely hopeless.

The Americans moved forward large numbers of reserves the following day, with the whole US VII Corps being thrown into the to-and-fro struggle, and they gradually gained ground. The 2nd Panzer Division put up the toughest resistance, defending every wooded area and every farm, but it was to no avail. After 48 hours, on the evening of 8 August, our forces had been pushed back to their jump-off positions. There was then a brief pause in the fighting.

The crisis at La-Lande-Vaumont

The LXXXIV Army Corps encountered severe difficulties in the meantime. As early as the assembly phase for the panzer thrust on Avranches, the enemy had started to assault the entire length of the front of the army corps. We learned from some of the prisoners we took that the US 28th Infantry Division had appeared on the battlefield. On the afternoon of 5 August, Lieutenant-General Elfeldt reported to his superiors via field telephone: 'It is the objective of the enemy to achieve a deep penetration on the right wing of the 363rd Infantry Division. The road junction at Vire is in immediate danger of being captured. Contact with the 3rd Parachute Division has been lost. The 353rd Infantry Division is holding its position at Champ-du-Boult and has taken 92 prisoners of war.' He decided to employ the 393rd Assault Gun Brigade to carry out a counter-thrust, and the enemy was compelled to fall back after 10 of his tanks had been put out of action.

The next major battle took place on 9 August. Between 0500 hours and 0600 hours, American artillery laid down heavy preparatory fire. Since the army corps had slightly withdrawn its front, most of the enemy shells fell harmlessly on the old foxholes. The point of main effort of the enemy attack was again the right wing of the 363rd Infantry Division. The Americans wanted at the same time to make headway along the Vire–Sourdeval and Vire–Tinchebray roads. After multiple costly attempts, their armoured spearheads reached the open terrain near La-Lande-Vaumont in the evening. There existed the very real threat of a breakthrough. The chief of staff of the army corps recalled the operationally destructive effect of a similar situation that had arisen on 26 July between Marigny and Gourfaleur, a repeat of which could not be allowed to occur. The headquarters of the army corps was therefore of the view that a second attack on Avranches would have to be postponed for the time being and that strong forces would need to remain in its sector to see to the elimination of the enemy at the point of penetration.

The enemy armoured spearheads had come to a stop. German forces launched a concentrated counter-attack the next morning from the east, south-east, and south. Since the British were carrying out holding attacks in the vicinity of Caen, the formation on our right, the II Parachute

Corps, was available to provide us with artillery support. This gave our counter-attack the necessary impetus to push forward, with the deepest penetration being achieved by the 984th Grenadier Regiment (of the 353rd Infantry Division). With that, there came a short respite.

On the following evening, the Seventh Army conducted a withdrawal so that it could shorten its front line and thereby release formations for its southern sector. This demanded of the enemy that he reassemble his troops before carrying out a new attack.

Holding attacks were executed by the Canadian First Army to the south of Caen early on 8 August for the purpose of supporting the Americans. It was the objective of the Canadians to break through the front between May-sur-Orne and Bourguébus and push forward in the direction of Falaise. This effort was preceded by an aerial bombardment carried out at 0430 hours by 1,000 four-engined enemy aircraft. Elements of the 272nd Grenadier Division and the whole of the 89th Infantry Division were struck with the full force of this bombardment. The latter formation had only just arrived from Norway. The conduct of battle of the Canadians caused us confusion. They mounted their infantry on the converted chassis of self-propelled guns and drove them through narrow alleyways so as to be able to plunge approximately five kilometres into the rear of the German position. The infantry would then dismount, fan out, and try to take strongpoints or battery positions from behind.

A new form of concentrated aerial bombardment known as box bombing tactics was employed by enemy aircraft along the approximately 10-kilometre curved front connecting Borguébus, Tilly, Rocquancourt, Fontenay, and May-sur-Orne. Mosquitoes marked the targets by dropping flares at midnight, and they were followed by approximately 450 heavy bombers. The hundreds of tonnes of explosives that fell cratered the terrain so extensively that it was impossible for the 12th SS Panzer Division Hitlerjugend to carry out any relief attacks. Within a few minutes, black clouds of smoke and dust blanketed the landscape. Seven hundred American bombers then flew overhead and struck the forwardmost row of strongpoints as well as the area behind them. They dropped high-explosive bombs that were designed to wipe out all life without leaving deep craters, for the Canadian armoured forces would

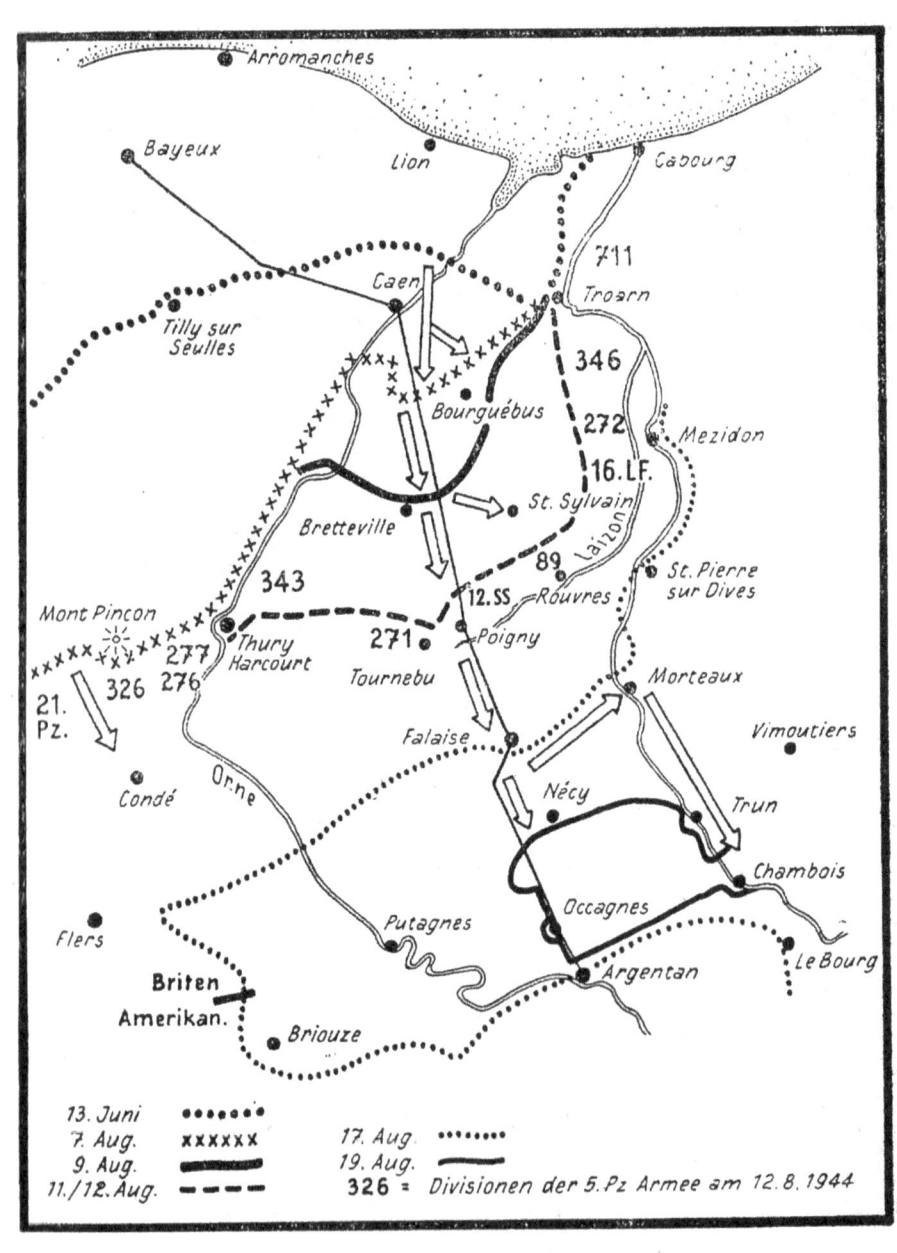

Map 14: Between Caen and Argentan

want to advance along an undamaged main road towards Falaise. Swarms of Typhoons put a stop to any movement of German vehicles, and they also targeted our flak units in an effort to eliminate our formidable 8.8cm anti-aircraft guns.

The retreat of the 89th Infantry Division was conducted with a degree of panic in some places, but there were other parts of the front that managed to hold on until noon. The Canadians regrouped at the line they had reached in readiness to renew the attack in the early afternoon. There were 600 enemy tanks, and they waited for the second wave of the box bombing before rolling forward! The number of enemy aircraft amounted to 1,400 four-engined bombers, 500 two-engined bombers, and 1,800 fighters and fighter-bombers. Although Bretteville fell into the hands of the Canadians, the enemy attack on the north bank of the Laison came to a sudden halt, as we had established a strong defensive position along the river. It was there that about 80 of our anti-aircraft guns and assault guns shot the approaching tanks of the Canadian 4th Armoured Division and Polish 1st Armoured Division to pieces. More than 150 of their steel monsters had been put out of action, and it is worth noting that this quantity exceeds the number of tanks we had been able to assemble for the operational counter-thrust at Mortain. The wrecks of the enemy vehicles lay before the well-camouflaged positions of our guns in a 5-kilometre semicircle, burning and smouldering in the fields. Such losses prevented the British infantry from making any further progress. The 343rd Grenadier Division, which had been detached from the Fifteenth Army, was moved forward so that it could strengthen the German defensive position. After that, the enemy attack remained motionless in front of the right wing of the Fifth Panzer Army.

We had achieved a great defensive success. Even though our panzer formations had fallen back further from Caen, it seemed as if the deadly threat to the north of Falaise had been eliminated. Now Field Marshal von Kluge was under pressure from the Führer's headquarters to carry out a second counter-thrust towards Avranches. To prepare for this, he shortened the front with a withdrawal to the Vire–Sourdeval–Mortain line and thereby made available some panzer formations. The fixation on pushing towards Avranches, an idea which on operational grounds ought to have been given up long ago, in tandem with the disregard for the danger posed by the US Third Army, which by that stage was already rolling towards Le Mans, was a clear invitation to the Americans to encircle our forces. It is therefore of no surprise that the US XV Corps set off on 10 August with the objective of thrusting deep into the open left flank of the German Seventh Army, heading towards Argentan via Alençon. On the northern flank, the Canadians continued their push on the Laison, and the result was that our front line increasingly resembled a wasp waist.

OB West assessed the situation on 8 August as follows:

> It is increasingly becoming apparent that the objective of the enemy, whose strength has in the meantime increased to at least 46 divisions, is Paris! With the British pushing towards Falaise and the Americans towards Le Mans, the enemy is striving to envelop the Seventh Army. The enemy is covering vast terrain in and committing many forces to this operation. A second major seaborne landing therefore seems unlikely, but it is quite probable that a major airborne landing will be conducted near the front with the idea of enabling a rapid thrust towards Paris. All available forces of Army Group B must be committed to the battlefront, and OB West has repeatedly requested of the OKW that it be permitted to send to that battlefront forces from other areas in the West. The panzer formations are to be assembled on the western wing of the Seventh Army for the renewed thrust on Avranches, although they remain far too weak in comparison with the highly mobile enemy forces.

The assessment concluded: 'Since the commencement of the invasion, 2,799 enemy tanks have been destroyed. Our losses have amounted to 148,075 men, amongst them 3,219 officers.'

During this time, the question of our rear positions in northern France became of increasing importance. OB West reported to the OKW on 7 August its intention to relieve the LXXXIV Army Corps, which had been engaged in heavy fighting ever since the first day of the invasion:

> The LXXXIV Army Corps will be placed at the disposal of the military commander in France for the preparation of our rear defensive positions, while the sector that had up until now been held by the LXXXIV Army Corps shall become the responsibility of the Wehrmacht commander in the Reich Commissariat of Belgium and Northern France. A reconnaissance headquarters will be formed from the command of Army Group D. The military commander in France and the garrison commander in Metz will be briefed accordingly.

On 10 August, Kluge recommended to the Operations Staff of the OKW that the second attack towards the west coast be postponed 'for the time being'. He was of the view that such an attack could not begin before 20 August and that the available forces should be committed to the conduct of a panzer thrust towards the south against the US XV Corps.

Events on the southern front meant that preparations had to be made quickly. The weak forces of the LXXXI Army Corps that stood there were only just enough to set up an obstacle line along the N807 highway from Mortain to Domfront via Barenton. Two-thirds of the panzer forces of this army corps were tied down in the vicinity of Mayenne, while the approaching elements of the 708th Infantry Division (Major-General Edgar Arndt) were easily overrun by the fully motorised American formations. The restoration of the situation was an absolute precondition for a renewal of the advance on Avranches.

General Eberbach was to be entrusted with this task. His Panzer Group Eberbach would be supported by the 9th Panzer Division (Major-General Erwin Jollasse), which was rolling forward from southern France. However, no matter how capable and energetic Eberbach was, these forces were far too weak to be able to ensure success. They were repeatedly struck by overwhelmingly superior enemy forces before they had a chance to assemble for the thrust that had been ordered, and Eberbach was compelled on each occasion to establish new defensive positions. Panzer Group Eberbach was detached from the Seventh Army on 18 August and made directly subordinate to Army Group B. Pushed back far to the east, it would now be responsible for the defence of Argentan, although there were several companies that did not reach the assembly area to the north of the Forêt d'Écouves in time due to the aerial superiority of the enemy. They had to find the best possible cover by day, and in so doing they lost all contact with the command posts of our formations. Our commanders, frequently under fire from enemy fighter-bombers, found and gathered the individual units so that they could at least set up some sort of defensive line. The combat strength of our formations decreased rapidly. By 14 August, for example, the size of the so-called 9th Panzer Division was no greater than that of a full-strength company. Our shortage of fuel meant that many of our tanks had to be abandoned and blown up.

With this description of the development of the situation on the southern front, it is possible that we have rushed on ahead of the events on other fronts, but the conclusion that can be drawn is that the attack that had been ordered in the Argentan–Alençon area had at best a small chance of success and only with the employment of all available panzer forces. OB West therefore approved a further withdrawal of the western front in Normandy on 14 August so that reinforcements could be made available for Panzer Group Eberbach. However, the new large-scale attack launched by the Canadians that same day in the direction of Falaise made the transfer of more panzer formations from the northern front, in particular that of the battle group of the 21st Panzer Division, impossible. The result was summarised in the war diary of OB West: 'Panzer Group Eberbach must go over to the defence for now. Should the decision be made to abandon the planned attack, the only possibility that remains is to try to break out from the pocket towards the north-east with all our forces. Such a decision must be taken without delay.'

The German panzer thrusts in the vicinity of Mortain were finally given up on 12 August. The reasons for and the consequences of the failure at Mortain were as follows:

1. The assembly of our troops had to be carried out with great haste and while in constant contact with the enemy.
2. The mountainous terrain of the 'Norman Switzerland' required that we concentrate our panzer forces in an area that was far too narrow. This circumstance, coupled with the limited allotment of fuel, rendered the panzer arm relatively immobile.
3. Flying weather had been good since noon on 7 August. This enabled enemy aircraft to maintain a presence in the air and to destroy much of our irreplaceable materiel. To await a period of poor weather would have been impossible due to the constantly changing situation at the front.

4. The concentration of almost all available combat vehicles at Mortain left the area to the south of Caen so exposed that it practically amounted to the abandonment of the northern front that had been defended so tenaciously since D-Day.
5. Finally, a whole week had been squandered, and the result was the conduct of a hasty withdrawal over a single bridge across the Orne in Putanges. It was inevitable that such a withdrawal would have a negative psychological impact on our troops. The attempt to rescue our remaining artillery pieces and combat vehicles placed considerable demands on our horse-drawn units, but the eventual destruction of much of the materiel of the Seventh Army could not be avoided.

Listed here are the formations at the front and their locations, from right to left, on 12 August 1944:

Army Group B

Advance command post, with elements of the 331st Infantry Division, in Gacé

Fifth Panzer Army

Headquarters in Meulles, to the north-east of Vimoutiers

(a) LXXXVI Army Corps with the 711th, 346th, and 272nd Infantry Divisions and the remains of the 16th Luftwaffe Field Division (coast–mouth of the Orne–Troarn–Saint-Sylvain)
(b) I SS Panzer Corps with the battle group of the 89th Infantry Division, the 12th SS Panzer Division Hitlerjugend, and 271st and 343rd Infantry Divisions (Saint-Sylvain–Grainville–Thury-Harcourt)
(c) LXXIV Army Corps with the 277th, 276th, and 326th Infantry Divisions and the battle group of the 21st Panzer Division (Thury-Harcourt–Mont d'Ancre–valley of the Druance near Lassy–Estry)

Boundary between the Fifth Panzer Army and Seventh Army: Chênedollé–Flers–La Ferté-Macé–Alençon

Seventh Army

Headquarters in Saint-André, to the south of Messei (near Flers)

(a) II Parachute Corps with the 3rd Parachute Division and the battle group of the Panzer Lehr Division (Chênedollé–Viessoix–Vire–valley of the Vire)
(b) LXXXIV Army Corps (headquarters in Saint-Jean-des-Bois, to the south-east of Tinchebray) with the 363rd Infantry Division, the battle groups of the 353rd and 331st Infantry Divisions, the 84th Infantry Division, and 116th Panzer Division (Saint-Germain–Vengeons–Sourdeval)
(c) XXXXVII Panzer Corps with the 2nd Panzer Division, elements of the 1st SS Panzer Division Leibstandarte SS Adolf Hitler, and elements of the 2nd SS Panzer Division Das Reich (Sourdeval–Mortain)
(d) LVIII Panzer Corps with the battle group of the 17th SS Panzer Grenadier Division Götz von Berlichingen, the 9th SS Panzer Division Hohenstaufen, and 10th SS Panzer Division Frundsberg (northern edge of the woods near Mortain–Domfront)
(e) LXXXI Army Corps (headquarters in Argentan) with the 708th Infantry Division, elements of the 5th Parachute Division, the 9th Panzer Division, and elements of the 1st Security Regiment (Domfront–valley of the Varenne–Mayenne–Sillé–Frenay)

By the time the order for the retreat across the Orne and the Dives was given, the Americans already stood before Alençon, a city renowned for its lace, and were thus approximately 75 kilometres to the east of the bulk of the German forces. We had to act as quickly as possible. In the days that followed, every formation had to conduct delaying actions by day and systematic withdrawal movements by night. The pocket, becoming ever smaller, gradually shifted from west to east.

Congestion on the roads meant that our horse-drawn units were unable to retreat quickly enough. They increasingly fell behind and, from 16 August, had only a handful of security units between them and the enemy spearheads. Vital road junctions and bridges were almost always subjected to the zone fire of medium and heavy artillery. He who disregarded the possibility of being attacked by low-flying aircraft and set off in the late afternoon while the roads were still empty had a chance of covering a reasonable distance before getting stuck behind countless trucks and horse-drawn vehicles. Traffic jams were typically 1 kilometre in length, and the vehicles in them moved forward at a snail's pace. Progress was hindered by partially destroyed bridges, damaged tanks occupying half the width of the roads, and sudden concentrations of artillery fire ripping our columns to shreds.

The night of 16/17 August was especially difficult, and long columns stood at dawn immediately before the blind curve leading to the deeply cut valley of the Orne and to the bridge in Putanges. Both the LXXXIV Army Corps and II Parachute Corps needed this bridge, which had barely been damaged, for their retreat across the river. It remains inexplicable as to why it had not been destroyed by enemy aircraft. Without this crossing, our route of retreat would have been cut off, and we would have had no choice other than to make use of narrow and not particularly viable temporary bridges made of barn doors.

Several events unfolded on 17 August. The British moved forward at two locations against our northern front with the idea of breaking through the salient. It was to either side of Mont Pinçon that the British Second Army applied pressure. Mont Pinçon itself, which lay to the south of the Odon, was the jump-off point. This dominant hill was 313 metres in height and had already been taken by the enemy at dusk on 6 August, though not before multiple British battalions had been shattered on the steep western slopes by the defensive fire of a battle group of the 326th Infantry Division. Enemy reconnaissance troops had eventually ascended the hill in thick fog, making use of several different paths, and had overpowered the last defenders in a single stroke. Now Mont Pinçon would serve as the observation post for the thrust on Condé and Tinchebray.

The Canadians had ground to a halt on 9 August, but it was with great tenacity that they resumed their efforts on 14 August to push forward between the Orne and the Dives in the direction of Falaise. In the valley of the Laison and in villages like Rouvres, Soumont, and Tournebu, fierce fighting raged and resulted in heavy casualties for both sides. Some 2,200 enemy bombers flew overhead in full daylight and without any regard for our anti-aircraft guns. Shortly thereafter, the Canadians penetrated our front line, which was held by only a few rear-guard units. By the evening, fighting was taking place in the streets of Falaise.

The 12th SS Panzer Division Hitlerjugend established an obstacle line to the south of the town and managed to hold its position behind it. The performance of this formation during the Allied invasion of Normandy was second to none. Places like Caen, Carpiquet, and the valley of the Orne have gone down in history thanks to the steadfastness and tenacity of the men and their commander, SS-Colonel Kurt 'Panzer' Meyer. If the area bombing and ground assaults conducted by the enemy caused any panic at all, it was always transformed into a wrathful repulse.

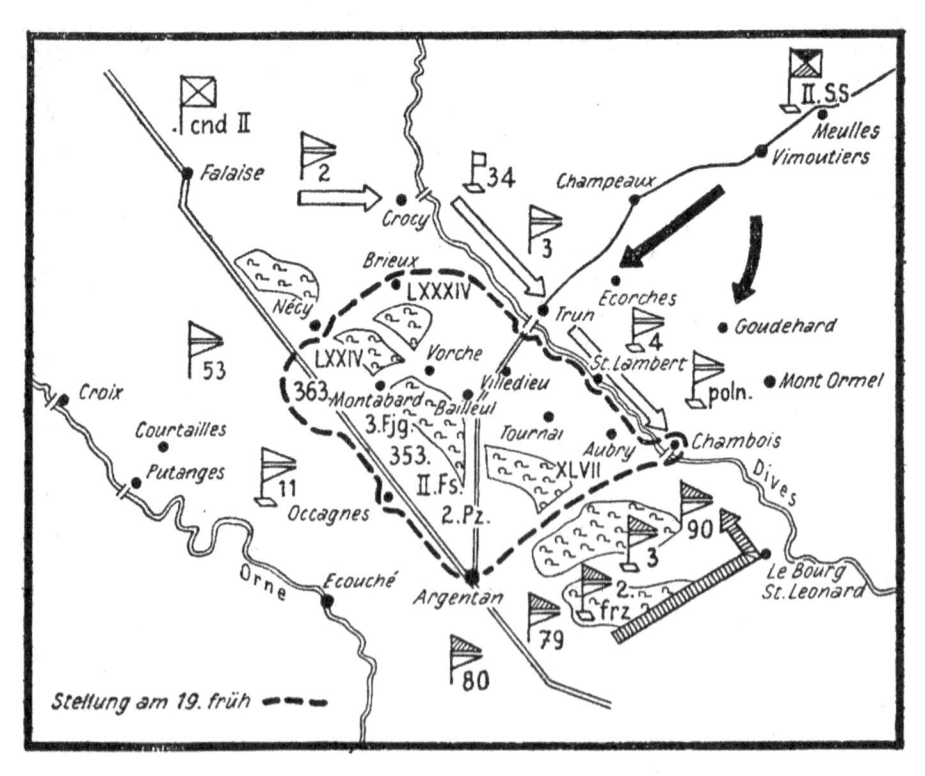

Map 15: The Falaise pocket

With the objective of sealing the pocket, the Canadian 4th Armoured Division and Polish 1st Armoured Division simultaneously crossed the Dives at Morteaux and advanced along the east bank of the river. In the meantime, the Americans had advanced beyond Briouze and occupied Argentan from the south. This meant that the Allied spearheads stood just 18 kilometres away from one another. German forces withdrew along the Putanges–Ri–Pierrefitte road towards Nécy on the night of 17/18 August. Enemy outposts were surprisingly nearby the entire time.

Two army and four corps headquarters all lay in close proximity to the towering church in Nécy. The precise nature of the situation was unclear: we knew neither the location of the enemy nor his strength. It took a few days for the intelligence section of the Seventh Army to produce a precise map of the enemy positions. We were also informed that Field Marshal von Kluge had been replaced by Field Marshal Model as commander of OB West.

CHAPTER 5

The last days in Normandy (18–21 August 1944)

The days from 18 until 21 August 1944 are engraved on the memories of those who took part in the fighting not so much because of the combat itself but rather due to the ever-shrinking pocket between the wooded areas of the Forêt de Gouffern and the marshy riverbed of the Dives. The remnants of our divisions were tested most severely as they attempted to break out of the pocket, and there were many cases where the order that had thus far been so well maintained descended into chaos.

    The II SS Panzer Corps, with the 8th and 9th Werfer Brigades, had already started to withdraw from the Argentan front on the morning of 17 August. It was to proceed to Lisieux and be put on standby. Falaise fell on the same day. The southern side of the pocket was held by strongpoints set up by the 116th Panzer Division, but the US 90th Infantry Division nevertheless succeeded in taking Le Bourg-Saint-Léonard. The bottleneck through which German forces could escape was barely 10 kilometres in width. For this reason, the order for the withdrawal of the II SS Panzer Corps was countermanded. Instead, it was to assemble at once on either side of Vimoutiers and execute a counter-thrust to the south west in the direction of Trun with the objective of keeping open the bottleneck for the retreat of the remaining elements of the Seventh Army and Fifth Panzer Army. The task to be carried out by General of Panzer Troops Heinrich Eberbach and his Fifth Panzer Army and by SS-General Wilhelm Bittrich and his II SS Panzer Corps would be full of difficulties. The main radio transmitters of our large formations were inoperative. The 1st SS Panzer Division Leibstandarte SS Adolf Hitler and 2nd SS Panzer Division Das Reich, still headed towards Lisieux, had come to a halt somewhere on the totally congested roads. Both generals and their orderly officers set off to find the divisional commanders. They diverted any units they came across, even the smallest ones, and then briefed the subordinate commanders of the completely mixed-up panzer formations at the command post of the II SS Panzer Corps near Meulles. It is of no surprise that it took most of our combat vehicles a long time to assemble, and only on 20 August could the counter-thrust be ventured.

The situation worsened considerably in the meantime. Canadian forces occupied Trun, which meant that the only places where we could cross the Dives were in Saint-Lambert and Chambois. With the pocket decreasing in size, the LXXXIV Army Corps, which had been involved in non-stop combat since the commencement of the invasion of Normandy, was finally relieved on the night of 17/18 August. Its headquarters, without any forces under its command, was placed at the disposal of the Seventh Army. However, on the very next day, this headquarters was given responsibility for all the forces on the northern front of the pocket. Lieutenant-General Otto Elfeldt, recognised for his unwavering composure, long experience at the front, and sober insight into what was within the realm of possibility, put all his energy into reorganising the mess of formations to the north. He succeeded in establishing a defensive line that ran from the vicinity of Trun to the area north of Rônai, via Ommoy and Brieux. The enemy applied pressure against this line primarily with artillery and low-flying aircraft. In the morning, the headquarters of the army corps received the news that no further help could be expected from units outside the pocket: every unit caught within it would have to rely on its own strength to break out. Strong German formations would have been needed to hold the front along the Eure against the pressure applied by the US Third Army. There existed the very real danger that another pocket would come into being around Rouen. We therefore had to act quickly!

Despite the glaring sunlight and enemy dominance of the skies, the army corps commenced its effort to break out at 1230 hours. It was an extremely risky course of action, but there was no other choice if the bulk of the army corps was to have a chance of making it to the east across the Dives. Unfortunately, with Bailleul as the objective that had been set, the leap to the east was not large enough. Our vehicles made the journey, rolling one behind the other, and progress was slow. Cursing the brilliant blue sky did not help, nor did wishing for mist, fog, or rain. If enemy aircraft darted towards us, most of the men ran to conceal themselves in the nearby grain fields. Groups of infantry troops lay in the roadside ditches and opened fire on the aircraft with their rifles or machine guns. Very rarely in the course of the invasion of Normandy were the enemy pilots presented with so many targets. Even so, there were surprisingly few enemy air strikes on this occasion, so our casualties on 18 August remained relatively low. This circumstance was somewhat mysterious to us. The Allied propaganda broadcaster *Soldatensender Calais* ('Soldiers' Radio Calais') spread rumours to the effect that attacks on our columns had simply stopped. The real reason was not known. Perhaps the thick clouds of dust thrown up by so many vehicles obscured visibility for the pilots of enemy aircraft, or maybe most of those aircraft had already been committed against the Seine and were leaving the rest of the work to the artillery.

Traffic congestion on the roads leading through the woods near Montabard was severe. Two or three columns moved alongside one another, and more columns wanted to join or even cross the slow flow of traffic. Smaller groups of troops made use of paths and secondary roads to overtake larger groups. 'The road is impassable,' protested a French forest ranger. Nevertheless, trucks and armoured vehicles squeezed onto or drove on either side of the road. After an hour, the damp forest ground was transformed into deep mud. Tree stumps damaged many of our vehicles. Our officers, with pistols drawn if necessary, obtained right of way on the main road for our artillery pieces and armoured vehicles, and saw to it that other vehicles gave way. On the other side of the woods, our troops would have to proceed through the Vorché–Bailleul–Villedieu area, which sloped down towards the Dives and which, by the following morning, would be exposed to the overlapping fire of enemy artillery from the north and south.

Despite these circumstances in the pocket, and despite the increasing certainty of our men that the last moment to evade death or capture had arrived, there was no widespread panic. There may have been a certain air of despondency, but discipline prevailed. Only in isolated cases might an exhausted man have suffered a mental breakdown. After night had fallen, the bulk of our retreating columns reached the burning village of Bailleul. Those who remained in the flow of the withdrawal movement, even without contact with their superiors, and those who reached and marched beyond their objective during the night somehow ended up outside the pocket the next morning, without quite knowing how they had done so. A front line? There were only roads to be followed towards somewhere further east.

On the morning of 19 August, the headquarters of the LXXXIV Army Corps received the following order: 'The army corps is relieved and is to assemble to the north of Mont-Ormel. After being replenished, it shall be employed in a new rear defensive position near Amiens.' This seemed rather grotesque in the current situation. The first general staff officer, Major Hasso Viebig, and the third general staff officer, Major Friedrich Hayn, met with the commander of the army corps, Lieutenant-General Otto Elfeldt, at 0700 hours. Bailleul lay below, barely recognisable through the smoke. The river meandered along the valley almost peacefully, but flashes on the horizon served as a reminder of the ever-approaching danger. The conference was brief and the mood was one of dejection, but we nevertheless focused on the task at hand. The quartermaster distributed the last of our rations. After a diet of turnips and cider, our dry army bread tasted splendid.

The front formed a rectangle, with the LXXXIV Army Corps holding the Trun–Brieux–Rônai sector, the LXXIV Army Corps the Neuvy–Tableauville sector, the II Parachute Corps the Pierrefitte–Occagnes sector, and the XXXXVII Panzer Corps the stretch from the northern part of Argentan to the high ground south of Trun via Chambois. The battle group of the 363rd Infantry Division was subjected to the heaviest enemy attacks. It stood in the middle of the salient beyond the Falaise–Argentan road and fiercely defended Rônai and Commeaux against multiple assaults launched by the British from the north and the Americans from the south. Its tremendous efforts enabled the other elements of the LXXXIV Army Corps to safely retreat to the east, and the battle group itself withdrew to Montabard at 1600 hours.

Although the Canadians only reached Saint-Lambert at noon, and although the Polish 1st Armoured Division only established contact with the Texans of the US 90th Infantry Division at 1900 hours, all the road junctions within the pocket had already come within the range of overlapping enemy artillery fire from 1030 hours. With the enemy batteries in position, the pocket was practically closed. It is highly likely that the enemy could have achieved this success as early as 18 August had a decisive thrust been executed by the American armoured forces, but Montgomery probably had not wanted the boundary between the Allied army groups to be crossed. The maintenance of this boundary gave many of our troops an opportunity to escape.

Artillery fire now rained down on every single one of our vehicles on the Trun–Villedieu–Argentan road. Enemy artillery observation aircraft hovered overhead and directed artillery fire onto units with as few as three or four men, and sometimes even individual messengers were targeted. Entire salvoes were fired at these small targets. Farmsteads on the outskirts of villages also came under fire from north, south, and east if any sort of movement was detected by the enemy. The ring of encirclement was being drawn tighter. Horse-drawn units proceeded across country as quickly as possible so that they could shelter in woods or depressions and await nightfall. Even field officers lacked a clear idea of how the situation was unfolding. All that was known was that the roads leading through the Forêt de Gouffern were completely blocked by columns that had been shot to pieces. The only way in which we could make further progress with our vehicles or heavy weaponry was to go through the barren terrain in the vicinity of Tournai.

Most of the enemy thrusts into the pocket were conducted from the south and west. The Canadians already had their hands full in exerting their control over the Dives crossings whilst also resisting the strikes launched by the II SS Panzer Corps into their deep flank. They avoided unnecessary casualties by falling back when we attacked and waiting on the gently undulating high ground to the east of the river. The Americans did the same near Chambois. The pocket was left to stew in its own juice for a while.

The battle groups break out of the pocket

The order for the night of 19/20 August read: 'Individual battle groups are to break out on their own. The remaining elements of the LXXXIV Army Corps will hold the northern front and will then disengage once the II Parachute Corps has withdrawn.' Given that the transmission of further orders would be technically impossible after the commencement of the breakout, each formation would be required to act on its own initiative. The events that followed were so varied and occurred in such quick succession that those involved in them could hardly grasp what was going on. Units that set off earlier managed to proceed from Saint-Lambert to Chambois without mishap, while those that left later encountered strong enemy forces and were compelled to fight their way out, suffering heavy casualties as they did so.

The 353rd Infantry Division made its way along a number of winding roads towards the east via Tournai. The village was ablaze, and its roads were blocked. Clearing-up operations delayed the withdrawal movement by hours. The quartermaster of the army corps fell in the vicinity of the church when a sudden concentration of enemy artillery fire occurred. The commander of the infantry division, Lieutenant-General Paul Mahlmann, personally scouted out the best roads to make use of, after which the bulk of his forces escaped the pocket via Moissy. The rest of his forces, positioned on the right wing, broke out in a single stroke immediately to the west of Chambois. The infantry division reassembled on the high ground near Mont-Ormel and then assumed responsibility for the defence of the Vie sector by establishing an obstacle line to the south-east in conjunction with parachute and SS units. Although the infantry division may not have had a long tradition, it brilliantly stood every test in Normandy from the first day to the last.

When the 3rd Parachute Division departed at 2230 hours, the divisional commander, Lieutenant-General Richard Schimpf, was severely wounded almost at once. The headquarters of the II Parachute Corps therefore

THE LAST DAYS IN NORMANDY (18–21 AUGUST 1944) • 127

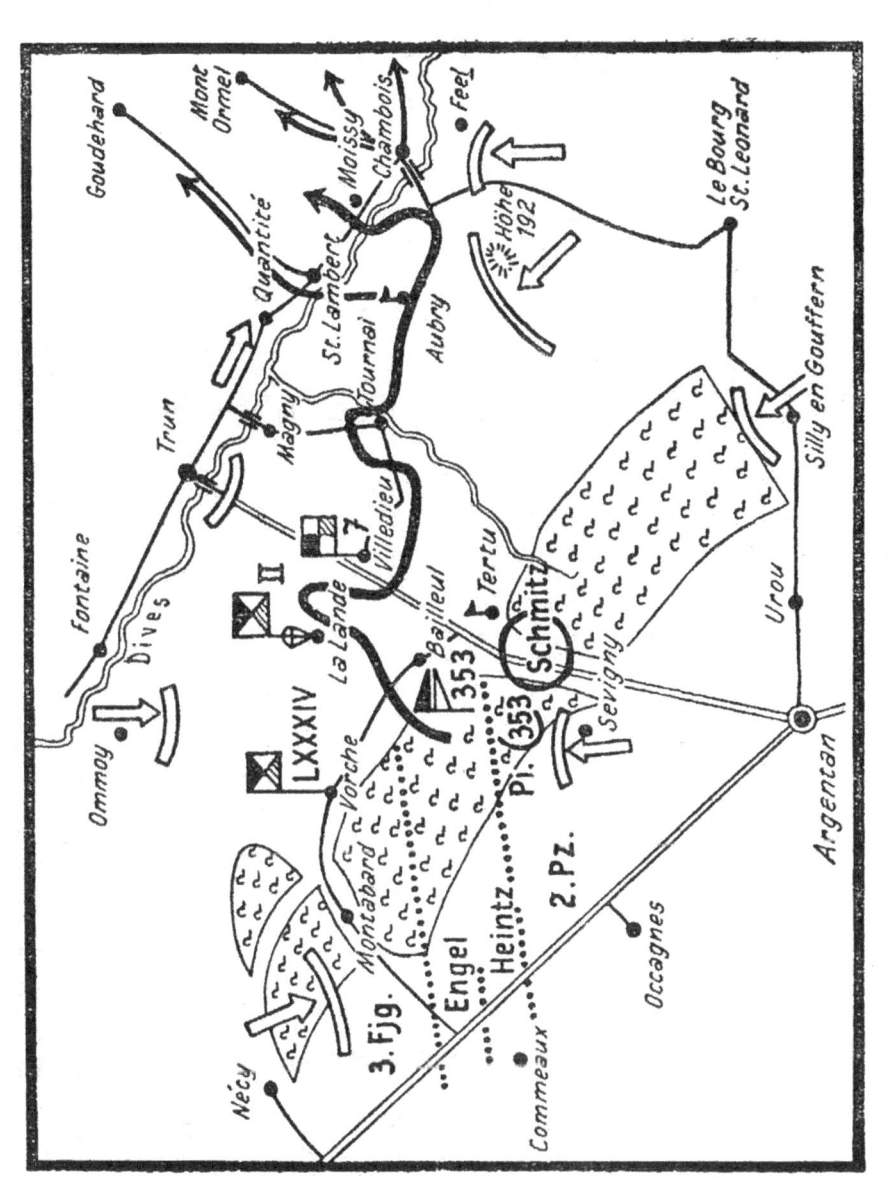

Map 16: The breakout of the 353rd Infantry Division

took charge of the conduct of the withdrawal, and the parachute troops slipped through the enemy armoured positions in small groups. Extensive reconnaissance was impossible, and navigation could only be done by compass. Exploiting any cover offered by the terrain, the parachute troops managed to avoid combat with the enemy. When dawn broke on 20 August, they took cover and only continued their march after dusk. With them was the commander of the Seventh Army, SS-General Paul Hausser, marching as an infantryman armed with a submachine gun. He was soon severely wounded by artillery fire, with a shell splinter almost ripping away his lower jaw. Even though most of the men of the parachute division were able to make it out of the pocket, there was by no means a large enough gap in the ring of encirclement to guarantee that the troops still within the pocket would be able to escape.

The chief of staff of the Seventh Army, Major-General Rudolf-Christoph Freiherr von Gersdorff, succeeded spectacularly in creating such a gap. He had been following Panzer Group Eberbach on the night of 19/20 August, but he had lost track of it and had discovered at 0400 hours that he was near the village of Saint-Lambert. Columns of vehicles had come to a halt at this village, which lay on the Trun–Chambois road, because much of the length of this road was controlled by the heavy fire of enemy anti-tank guns. Gersdorff brought two damaged tanks of the 2nd Panzer Division into action and destroyed those anti-tank guns. Our columns then crossed the road and escaped through the gap that had been made in the enemy front, and that was the signal for the forces still inside the pocket to rush towards that gap. Several scout cars, tanks, and assault guns broke cover and drove towards one of the positions of the US 90th Infantry Division. The American troops in that position were completely taken by surprise. They surrendered immediately, although the German troops were unable to do anything with them. They were therefore disarmed and simply left where they were. When the fragments of the divisions that had escaped the pocket had a chance to stop, Gersdorff, with the assistance of some energetic officers from the 116th Panzer Division and 12th SS Panzer Division Hitlerjugend, reorganised them into a new battle group. Once it had properly assembled and conducted reconnaissance, it continued the push to the east. Gersdorff drove back into the pocket to look for Hausser, and he found him in a long line of soldiers marching out. News of the gap had spread. It was, and remained, the focal point of the breakout.

At 0700 hours on 20 August, the XXXXVII Panzer Corps, elements of which were already working in conjunction with other battle groups, reached the area between Saint-Lambert and Chambois with the bulk of the 1st SS Panzer Division Leibstandarte SS Adolf Hitler and 2nd Panzer Division. The bold breakout that had been executed by the 353rd Infantry Division and the troops under Gersdorff's leadership triggered heavy enemy barrage fire of the kind that had not yet been seen during the entire campaign. Our reconnaissance revealed that the road through Moissy, which lay immediately to the north-west of Chambois, offered the best cover and was therefore the safest to use. It was along this road that groups of German troops, one after the other, proceeded to safety, and they suffered relatively few casualties in so doing. The 2nd Panzer Division, commanded by the wounded Lieutenant-General Heinrich Freiherr von Lüttwitz, fought tooth and nail to ensure the security of the route of retreat. Only on the night of 20/21 August did approximately 50 combat vehicles belonging to the 116th Panzer Division make it out of the pocket. The group of this panzer division that had been committed on the southern front against the Americans in the vicinity of Argentan since 14 August lost all radio contact with the rest of our forces, and it was not long before the troops allocated to that group were taken prisoner.

The remaining forces of the LXXXIV Army Corps held the northern front while the other battle groups inside the pocket tried to break out. British forces applied considerable pressure from the west. As fate would have it, the army corps would be not only the first German formation to have been involved in the fighting in Normandy but also the last. This was because the army corps was to exit the pocket only after the parachute troops had done so. The night went by agonisingly. We received no news whatsoever about how much progress was being made by the parachute troops. It was already 0300 hours, and Lieutenant-General Elfeldt decided to set off on foot at the head of the few forces at his disposal. However, at Saint-Lambert, his almost defenceless forces clashed with a fully prepared combat command of the Polish 1st Armoured Division. Encircled in a narrow pass, the German troops suffered heavy casualties and were eventually taken prisoner. Out of a total of 20 senior headquarters that had been encircled, those of the LXXXIV Army Corps and the 84th Infantry Division were the only ones that did not make it out.

All of the groups that were already in position near the Dives on the morning of 20 August benefited from the counter-thrust that was executed by the II SS Panzer Corps at 1000 hours. Committed to this counter-thrust were 25 combat vehicles and three battalions. However, both roads of advance were so significantly obstructed by exhausted troops or abandoned vehicles that the SS tanks had to roll through an alleyway instead. An overcast sky denied low-flying aircraft full visibility. The thrust from the area on either side of Vimoutiers into the Canadian and Polish flank resulted in a successful advance of several kilometres and brought the high ground of Coudehard, Écorches, and Les Champeaux into our possession. There was thus a momentary relief of pressure that allowed 20,000 men, 25 tanks, and 60 guns to escape the pocket that morning. These were surprisingly high numbers. Unfortunately, troops of ours that were further to the west missed this last opportunity to withdraw. They had been forced to take cover against enemy aircraft and artillery and remained unaware of the SS relief attack on the other side of the Dives.

The third general staff officer of the LXXXIV Army Corps had been lacking in any sort of contact with the formation headquarters ever since the early morning of 20 August. Accompanied by an orderly officer, he was stuck in the middle of a column of horse-drawn vehicles. His car lay with a broken axle in the vicinity of Tournai. He arrived a short distance from Chambois and had just come up behind a damaged tank when the column was scattered by enemy barrage fire. Most of our vehicles fell back, circled around, and reassembled in the afternoon in the grounds of the Château de Bas Aubry. Any further movement was impossible due to constant enemy fire. Our men found refuge in the solid, medieval round tower of the aristocratic estate. Barely 1.5 kilometres away, numerous enemy reconnaissance and combat vehicles drove back and forth along the high-lying road connecting Saint-Léonard, Fougy, and Chambois and secured a main line of resistance. Our men were exhausted and, in some cases, wounded. We possessed no tanks and few small arms. Any attempt at a breakout would have to be carried out across lowlands filled with ditches. The situation seemed to be completely hopeless.

All our efforts turned towards taking care of the wounded. They and the medical personnel who tended to them had been sheltering in woods, near narrow valleys, and in farmhouses that had been shot to pieces. Many more wounded men, receiving no attention at all, lay on the roads and were covered in blood and dust. The central part of the château was quickly set up as an assembly point for the wounded, and white sheets displaying the Red Cross sign were to be seen on the lawn of the forecourt. A radio car in the park announced the location of the field hospital, but the enemy failed to pick up this message. Perhaps our signals were too weak, or maybe there was too much radio traffic to keep track of. Either way, the bombardment of the building and the surrounding area continued unabated.

By the early hours of 21 August, the Americans were standing in the château courtyard. Those who were unable to fight were handed over to a captain of the US 90th Infantry Division and were soon being looked after by American medical personnel. In the meantime, the third general staff officer had made it through the enemy lines. He had concealed himself in rows of bushes and had slipped past the Texan infantry. One American, perhaps an emigrant from Germany, quietly played '*Ach, du lieber Augustin, alles ist hin!*' on his harmonica.[1] Left behind were many dead comrades from the fighting in Normandy; but no man is truly left behind if he is not forgotten!

---

1   Translator's note: 'Ach, du lieber Augustin, alles ist hin!' ('Oh, you dear Augustin, all is lost!') was a popular melancholic Viennese song.

CHAPTER 6

General observations

The conduct of battle in the hedgerow countryside

The nature of the terrain in Normandy greatly shaped the conduct of battle by both sides. In particular, the topography was such that the Allies were able to fully exploit their aerial superiority.

Prior to the commencement of the invasion, there existed a more or less continuous main line of resistance along the coast. In close proximity to the beach, this main line of resistance consisted of small and large strongpoints. The distance between these fortifications had been chosen so that each lay within visual range of the next. The local commanders had been issued with written instructions as to how they were to conduct battle, and the fortifications themselves had been stocked with rations and ammunition. Those stocks were enough for small strongpoints to last one week and for large ones to last three weeks.

German forces had been organised flexibly behind the main line of resistance. So that it would be possible for local reserves to be created, the strongpoints had been garrisoned by only small numbers of personnel while the detached troops had been concentrated into mobile standby units. When Field Marshal Erwin Rommel took command of the coastal front, he rescinded this measure in favour of larger garrisons in the strongpoints: 'The main line of resistance is the coast!'

Once the invasion was underway, prominent landmarks further inland were occupied if they offered a good view of the surrounding terrain or if they enabled enemy penetrations to be outflanked. Considerable portions of the terrain that lay in between those landmarks remained unoccupied. The gaps were covered with great success by our artillery units, specifically by the concentrated, overlapping fire of neighbouring batteries. Wherever our front line was located, it followed wherever possible the marshy banks of streams or the muddy ground of lowlands. Such terrain offered the defender highly effective anti-tank ditches.

The combat zone was the hedgerow countryside of Normandy, an undulating landscape overgrown with bushes and interspersed with apple orchards or grazing areas. This terrain favoured the defence that would be conducted by the LXXXIV Army Corps and therefore compensated somewhat for the numerical superiority enjoyed by the enemy in tanks and aircraft. The many hedgerows, roughly one metre in height and made up of lines of bushes or trees, divided the terrain into hundreds of small rectangles. Especially important for our defence were a number of low-lying narrow gullies, most of which were completely concealed by greenery. They formed natural fire trenches and permitted the safe movement of troops by day.

Bushes and trees made it difficult for the enemy to properly observe the effect of his preparatory artillery fire. From the point of view of the enemy, the success of any bombardment was in doubt unless there was an enormous expenditure of ammunition. The degree of any such success was reduced by the fact that American shells, possessing highly sensitive detonators, tended to explode in treetops. Furthermore, American artillery observers often accompanied the first wave of infantry troops in the early days of the invasion of Normandy, but after suffering heavy casualties, they switched to sitting in the tanks that paved the way for the attack spearheads.

Our infantry units were generally forced to fight defensively. The men lodged themselves in narrow gullies or foxholes and positioned their machine guns and mortars so that other narrow gullies and gaps in rows of hedges could be covered by fire. Particular attention was paid to covering the gates between fields. Every combat unit, no matter how small, made preparations that would allow it to exploit or bypass natural obstacles. For example, small pathways were cut into the rows of bushes so that our men would be able to disappear quickly and without being noticed.

There was one factor that proved to be decisive for our defensive success, and that was the performance of our combat troops. The visual range offered by the terrain was limited to only 100 to 150 metres. It was therefore impossible for any single commander to observe a large stretch of the front line. Defensive sectors were echeloned, but there often existed little contact between neighbouring units. Those units were compelled to withdraw whenever the enemy struck the flanks or applied pressure in close combat. Since our officers could not be everywhere at once, it was up to our non-commissioned officers and enlisted men to conduct themselves in accordance with the training they had received for combat in the hedgerow countryside. They stood this test with honour. Discipline, tenacity, and strength of character prevailed time and again. Even though the propulsive momentum of victory after victory was long gone, and the old feeling of the invincibility of the German Army had faded away, the inner fabric of our regiments remained intact.

The hedgerow countryside and apple orchards of Normandy

The situation was worse for the American riflemen. Despite their strong and well-prepared attacks, they often ran into trouble. Heavy casualties gnawed at their morale. A single German machine gun was enough to make a medium-sized American formation proceed with caution. A single German unit, acting decisively, could tie down such a formation. The American infantrymen tried to avoid close combat in Normandy. They had great respect not only for our heavy machine guns and mortars but also for our 8.8cm anti-aircraft guns, which we frequently used against ground targets.

The enemy sought to fully exploit his qualitative and quantitative superiority in materiel. His infantry possessed better weaponry than ours. Specifically, his troops were abundantly equipped with the most modern mechanical and automatic weapons. Tanks always accompanied the enemy infantrymen, and machine guns were mounted on those tanks so that they could fire over the hedges.

The role of tanks

The terrain was favourable for defensive combat against tanks. Even smaller weapons like anti-tank rifles and anti-tank rocket launchers could be used, although such weapons were only effective at close range. Their employment in close combat was dependent on opportunities arising for the destruction of enemy tanks and on men being available for firing the weapons. These two factors did not always coincide.

Tanks were prevented from making full use of their mobility on the Cotentin Peninsula. Most of the countryside roads were too narrow, made as they had been for local and farming traffic. The soil underneath and on either side of those roads was deep, and this made it difficult for vehicles to spread out or to overtake one another. If the tanks at the head of a column got stuck in mud, damaged by mines, or destroyed by direct hits, the resulting wrecks became roadblocks for the following vehicles. Nevertheless, the monstrosities of steel remained decisive offensive weapons for the Americans. The enemy tanks initially acted as tactical instruments that provided support in attack and defence. After the breakthrough at Avranches, however, the time had come for them to serve as operational weapons: they had become what would have been in times past the army's cavalry.

Our tanks were superior to those of the enemy in terms of armour and armament. Their extra-long 7.5cm guns were outstanding. However, the local conditions backfired on us, for the superb firing range of our Panthers was negated by restricted manoeuvrability and visibility in the combat zone. Any counter-thrusts we launched ground to a halt and resulted in heavy casualties. As an American prisoner of war commented: 'The best way to weaken the Germans was to get them to counter-attack.'

Two further circumstances had an unfavourable effect on the panzer arm. Enemy aircraft forced our repair sections to be kept well back. Because of this, it was often impossible to tow and repair tanks that had been rendered immobile, so they were buried in the ground instead as makeshift bunkers. They were thus permanently robbed of their souls – their mobility – and had to be abandoned altogether whenever we were compelled to retreat. On top of this, the panzer divisions rarely had a chance to pause and regroup. They were constantly employed for putting out fires, such as plugging gaps in the front, intercepting enemy thrusts head-on, or regaining territory by striking the enemy flank. The non-stop enemy attacks denied us the time we needed to concentrate our panzer forces and conduct an operational counter-thrust. Each time we used the panzer arm to deal with emergencies, the enemy was given the opportunity to further strengthen his hold on Normandy. Many of our tanks were left where they were due to fuel shortages or technical problems, having quite literally been marched to death.

The Americans developed a form of combat in the hedgerow countryside which we referred to as chessboard tactics. Viewed from the air, the landscape resembled a chessboard with its thousands of quadrilateral fields and orchards. Each of those quadrilaterals measured approximately 100 by 150 metres, and the enemy spearhead moved forward field by field. The Americans employed specially trained combat teams made up of armoured, pioneer, artillery, and infantry troops. The attack would commence with artillery and fighter-bombers ploughing up the area in and around the objective. Pioneer troops would then blow holes through the hedges to enable the tanks to roll into the field, and the units that followed eliminated any remaining German resistance. Once all the American infantrymen had arrived, the combat team regrouped and repeated the process.

These chessboard tactics were by no means a case of gaining attack momentum and moving forward rapidly. They consisted of taking possession of small sectors that had been thoroughly bombarded beforehand. Even more so than in World War I, it was the use of modern technology that characterised the conduct of warfare by the Americans in Normandy. They relied on their equipment so that their men could be spared bloodshed. The psychological and physical demands placed on the German soldier, by comparison, were far greater. Despite our defeat in Normandy, our men had demonstrated that they could bear the heaviest of burdens.

The enemy's aerial supremacy

The aerial supremacy enjoyed by the enemy lasted throughout the course of the invasion of Normandy. So much so did enemy aircraft concentrate their efforts there that the Allied bombing campaign against the Reich itself abated somewhat. The aircraft of the US Eighth and Ninth Air Forces and RAF Bomber Command were committed both operationally as long-range weapons and tactically for close support. They were also used for the conduct of aerial reconnaissance, ensuring constant observation of the front along its entire length.

Aside from hunting for German vehicles on the roads of Normandy, enemy fighter-bombers were employed for the support of armoured spearheads. These light machines were the eyes of enemy tanks that were rolling forward. Whenever six or so fighter-bombers were circling overhead, we knew that enemy forces must be approaching. The fighter-bombers attacked any obstacles we had set up and eliminated any anti-tank guns we had positioned on the flanks.

Most dangerous were the box bombing tactics of Allied bombers against our ground positions so as to create the conditions for a breakthrough. This method was first developed by the British in the wake of the heavy casualties they had suffered to the south of Caen, where so many of their armoured and infantry attacks had ground to a halt due to the effectiveness of our defensive fire. The Americans would then commit between 1,500 and 2,000 medium and heavy bombers whenever they wanted to tear open a narrow sector of our front. This was the case, to name just a few examples, on 1 July at Caumont, on 18 July during the attempted envelopment of Saint-Lô, and on 25 July during the attack over the Lessay–Périers road.

When the LXXXIV Army Corps reported for the first time that 1,500 enemy aircraft had been committed against a small sector held only by a battalion, nobody at the Seventh Army could believe it. The news was regarded as sheer exaggeration, and there was even some annoyance that a headquarters so well regarded for its level-headed assessments would now try to overstate the seriousness of the situation. The chief of staff of the Seventh Army, Major-General Max Pemsel, queried the report by telephone. Despite being given the same details, he decided to halve the reported number when passing on the information. The headquarters of the Seventh Army took the view that if the original number was correct, not even a mouse would have survived in the sector that had been hit.

It is difficult to describe the effect of the enemy area bombing and carpet bombing. The ground had been struck again and again. The thickest tree trunks had snapped like matches. Tanks, trucks, and guns had been tipped over into or against the sides of bomb craters. Most of the defenders were covered with debris. Those who survived dug themselves out, but only once the sounds of detonating bombs had faded away. They looked for their small arms, tried to reposition their artillery pieces, and searched for ammunition, but it was often the case that they were still defenceless by the time the enemy appeared.

Our troops were often surprised to see Allied aircraft taking off and landing nearby. Temporary airfields seemed to be multiplying rapidly, the explanation for which we discovered later. The enemy constantly constructed landing strips close to the front by laying portable metal surfaces on level areas. The Americans also developed a technique of clearing away fog around their airfields by pumping petroleum into pipes perforated with thousands of tiny holes. The resulting flames warmed the air and caused the fog to lift.

Provided the weather was good, the Luftwaffe undertook approximately 250–300 sorties per day in the Caen sector. Our aircraft usually conducted surveillance behind our own lines by day or laid mines along the coast at night. Opposite the American sector, the LXXXIV Army Corps received no air support whatsoever. Even if, in response to multiple requests, a firm promise was made by the Luftwaffe to provide air support, it was always the case that such assistance failed to materialise. No notification was ever given. This was what happened, for example, on 13 June when the 17th SS Panzer Grenadier Division Götz von Berlichingen launched its attack on Carentan. It was of no use to us to be informed afterwards that German aircraft were unable to break through enemy defences and that this was because the Americans, thanks to the excellence of their radio and measurement technology, were able to discern and commit fighters against our flight path even before our aircraft were properly airborne.

Our grievances finally reached the Führer's headquarters in far-distant East Prussia. A request was made of the headquarters of the LXXXIV Army Corps to provide a more detailed report on the situation in the air in Normandy. We were able to report that a grand total of seven German aircraft had appeared in the skies over the combat zone of the army corps in the month of June. To be absolutely clear, that means that the Luftwaffe committed just seven aircraft against the entire American sector at that time. It took a great deal of effort on our part to have this fact officially reported, and it was particularly frustrating for us that the information gathered from ground reconnaissance, spy reports, prisoner-of-war statements, and captured maps tended to lose its value the higher up the chain of command it went. The supreme command, so far away as it was from the front, led the German forces as if it were conducting military exercises.

Signals technology

American signals technology was much better than ours. The units of the enemy possessed small, easily portable, high-quality radio and telephone equipment. This equipment was distributed right down to squad leaders and reconnaissance units so that communications could be maintained and orders conveyed, even at night, in the impenetrable hedgerow countryside. Radio communications between infantry and armoured units, between armoured and artillery observation posts, and even between ground troops and observation aircraft were of a high standard.

The radio equipment at the disposal of the German infantry divisions was inadequate, and the state of communications at lower levels of command was worse. The equipment used by our battalions was heavy and difficult to set up.

In contrast, our signals intelligence units had achieved some notable successes, working in close cooperation with the well-equipped reconnaissance stations of the Luftwaffe. By studying captured documents, the leadership of the German Army in the West managed to crack the code used by the Allied air forces. This enabled us to decode the radio messages of the enemy in the weeks that followed. Every evening, the headquarters of the army corps was able to inform the divisions under its command of the areas that were going to be bombed and of any other sorties that were going to be flown by enemy aircraft. We even knew most of the time where and when the enemy planned to carry out aerial photography. The tactical objectives of the enemy for the following day could be identified, and warnings were quickly sent to the subordinate units that were in danger. This gave the units in question sufficient time to shift their positions.

The practice of command

Under the command of Field Marshal Erwin Rommel, Army Group B was responsible for the formations along the coast that awaited the enemy invasion. It was headquartered in La Roche-Guyon, on the Seine north-west of Paris, and was subordinate to OB West (formerly Army Group D), which was commanded by Field Marshal Gerd von Rundstedt and headquartered in Saint-Germain-en-Laye and then Paris. This division of responsibilities caused some surprise at the headquarters of the LXXXIV Army Corps.

We regarded Rundstedt – the victor in Poland, France, and southern Russia – as the ideal field commander. A reserved individual, he was a venerable representative of the old army. We could hardly imagine why there was any need for a division of authority, in this case the insertion of an additional headquarters between that of Army Group D and those of the armies that had been under its command. Experiences of subdividing the front in Russia were not applicable to France, for the terrain was nowhere near as vast.

The division of command resulted in a clash of ideas over the conduct of battle. Rommel, though he had been promoted and had been given greater responsibilities by the OKW, predominantly thought tactically. This is demonstrated by his remark that the main line of resistance had to be along the coast. The forces at the front had originally been organised into small strongpoints and detached mobile standby units, but he countermanded this and saw to it that each strongpoint was fully occupied and each artillery piece was pointed towards the sea. In contrast, Rundstedt thought much more operationally. It was his opinion that an Allied landing, due to the superiority of the enemy at sea and in the air, could not be prevented. He therefore wanted most of his forces to be kept in reserve for a counter-strike against a successful landing. He favoured mobile rather than static defence and thus called for the panzer divisions to remain on standby to the rear.

While this contrast might be somewhat exaggerated, it highlights the different approach of these two commanders. Rommel knew from his time in Africa of the decisive influence of Allied aerial superiority. He rejected the idea of hurling operational reserves from great distances at points of penetration. Given the way in which the situation unfolded, he was undoubtedly correct in this regard. On the other hand, the bombing raids of 6 June targeted our strongpoints and shattered much of the strength of our divisions. Since our defence in depth was lacking, even minor penetrations of the front threatened to develop into major breakthroughs. Nevertheless, something good did come out of the contest of opinions, and that was the detachment of reserves that were kept close to the front.

Our doubts about the necessity of the insertion of Army Group B soon dissipated. Rommel and the formations at his disposal became actively involved in the construction of coastal defences. There were many tasks to be carried out and positions to be manned, and we realised that the fight at the front might indeed have to draw on the forces of an entire army group. OB West would have enough on its plate, remaining as it did in charge of all German forces in France: its responsibilities included two army groups, three military administrative bodies, and coordination with the navy and the Luftwaffe.

A second circumstance in the practice of command turned out to be much more momentous, and that was the intervention of the OKW in the conduct of operations. It repeatedly ordered that every single point be held, and required that any decision to disengage or withdraw had to be approved by the Führer's headquarters before being carried out. This interference by the OKW extended into the operational and even tactical realms, even influencing the employment of regiments and the use of roads. What was most alarming, however, was that the OKW rarely took into consideration the actual situation at the front. We occasionally managed to ignore orders issued by the supreme command, but the overall effect of its constant exertion of control was damaging.

The Seventh Army and LXXXIV Army Corps became mere recipients of orders. Never had our general staff officers been so disempowered or deprived of freedom of action. Even the battalion commanders were furious about the conditions under which their corps commander had to lead. The insistence on strictly following orders that had been made from above had disastrous consequences. Examples of this from the fighting in Normandy include the commitment of four divisions to the Cherbourg area, the pointless presence of the reinforced 319th Infantry Division on the Channel Islands, and the panzer thrust at Mortain. A prime example of the disastrousness of the interference of the OKW, though, is its continued belief that the main Allied landing would take place in the Pas-de-Calais. Forces that could have been transferred to Normandy were instead kept where they were. It is a historical truth that Hitler, though his planning in various theatres of war had been ingenious, tended to waste his trump cards.

A third circumstance in the practice of command must be mentioned, namely the system of parallel headquarters that functioned independently from one another. Even within one combat zone, the three branches of the Wehrmacht were led by different centres of command. Each branch led an almost special existence at a time when all our resources needed to be coordinated for a concerted effort. No army commander could issue orders to another branch of the Wehrmacht if the situation was not, in the narrowest sense, considered to be critical. To allow this would have been regarded as inappropriate, for what applied to the party and the way in which it was organised also applied outside the realm of politics, and that was that no overwhelmingly strong concentration of power could be permitted. Nevertheless, cooperation between the lower levels of command and between the units at the front was perfectly comradely. The urgency of the situation often ensured that inter-service rivalries were put aside.

The physically exhausted Colonel-General Friedrich Dollmann, commander at the headquarters of the Seventh Army in Le Mans, suffered a heart attack on the morning of 28 June. This distinguished commander had been unable to cope with the events that followed the successful Allied landings, especially when the chief of the OKW, Field Marshal Wilhelm Keitel, was prompted by the fall of Cherbourg on 26 June to initiate an investigation into the measures that had been taken by Dollmann and his advisers against the invasion. General of Artillery Edgar Theisen and General Judge Henning Freiherr von Beust were entrusted with the task of carrying out the investigation. Dollmann remained unaware that he had, despite Rommel's objections, been relieved of command by Hitler.

Dollmann was replaced by SS-General Paul Hausser, who had previously been commander of the II SS Panzer Corps. He was the first member of the Waffen-SS to be placed in command of a field army. He had served in the interwar German Army and was the commander of Infantry Command IV when he retired in 1932. He subsequently became the inspector of the SS combat troops, and, as one of the most qualified officers in the Waffen-SS, led an SS motorised division and then an SS panzer corps during the first few years of the war.

SS-General Hausser was an outstanding soldier and human being. He soon gained recognition not only for his courage under fire, exposing himself to much more danger than would ordinarily be expected from someone in his position, but also for his frequent visits to the men at the front. His commitment as a commander and his care for his troops were combined with unparalleled modesty and amiability.

We at the headquarters of the LXXXIV Army Corps hoped that Hausser would be able to use his influence to bring about the full implementation of mobile resistance. He possessed better insight than his superiors and was even prepared to criticise their opinions, although he had become *persona non grata* since his isolated SS panzer corps had evacuated Kharkov in 1943 against the explicit orders that had been issued and repeated by Hitler. As was the case with all German commanders, his sense of honour as a soldier stood in striking contrast to the political atmosphere that prevailed at the time. He felt the tension between the obedience demanded of him by his superiors and the loyalty he demonstrated to the Fatherland and to the men under his command. He was a true representative of the military ethos of the old school. He did everything possible that was within his powers: he ordered the Seventh Army, against Hitler's will, to break out of the Falaise pocket, an extraordinarily great risk to take in the wake of the events of 20 July 1944. To the problem of the interference of the OKW in any disengagement, he found a solution of striking simplicity. When Choltitz expressed his frustration on one occasion over having to await the approval of the OKW for the conduct of a withdrawal, Hausser said to him: 'You can simply report that you were thrown out of your position, and it will become a *fait accompli*.'

On 29 July, when Major-General Pemsel was posted to Norway, Colonel Rudolf Christoph Freiherr von Gersdorff became the new chief of staff of the Seventh Army. He had taken part in the campaign in France in 1940 as the first general staff officer of the 86th Infantry Division and had then served as the liaison officer with the Abwehr in the intelligence section of Army Group Centre during the campaign in Russia from 1941. He had become the chief of staff of the LXXXII Army Corps in the Pas-de-Calais in January 1944, and it was from there that he had then been transferred to the Seventh Army.

Fortresses

The OKW greatly overestimated the value of our so-called fortresses. It believed, despite our experiences in Stalingrad and Crimea, that they would serve as wave-breakers in Normandy and Brittany and thereby tie down many of the troops belonging to the invasion forces. This was a mistake. While the heavy casualties suffered by the Americans at Saint-Malo deterred them from attempting a rapid conquest of the fortress, they contented themselves with cutting it off and awaiting its surrender.

The fate of the 319th Infantry Division on the Channel Islands was quite typical. The strength of this formation far exceeded what was normal during wartime. It had at its disposal a panzer battalion, a well-equipped flak brigade, several pioneer and naval units, and nine naval batteries with 32 guns. Multiple requests made by the Seventh Army for the transport of these forces to the mainland were rejected, and the infantry division had received many nicknames even before the commencement of the invasion, including 'The Skat Club', 'POW Camp Guernsey', and 'The King's Own German Grenadiers'. With a strength of approximately 30,000 men, it carried out no more than a few minor raids on Granville in March and April 1945. It depleted its rations and surrendered in May 1945 without resistance.

In Brittany, the situation was somewhat different. Throughout the course of the invasion, five divisions were sent from there to Normandy (the 3rd and 5th Parachute Divisions and the 77th, 275th, and 353rd Infantry Divisions). Four divisions remained in Brittany, but even they handed over strong battle groups – generally reinforced regiments – to the LXXXIV Army Corps. The two corps in Brittany (the XXV and LXXIV Army Corps) were so significantly weakened by this shift of forces that they were no longer capable of effectively defending the coast. It is worth noting that the surveillance of and the fight against the French Resistance drew upon the troops of many of our units. However, on the orders of the supreme command, our fortresses were not permitted to be reduced in strength. The garrisons of those fortresses were precisely stipulated and were composed of elements from all branches of the Wehrmacht. Consequently, the Seventh Army ordered that our defensive efforts in Brittany were to be restricted to these fortresses and that the coastal sectors lying in between them were only to be monitored. The bulk of our weaponry that had previously been positioned outside the fortresses – coastal artillery, infantry support guns, and anti-aircraft guns – were moved so that they would lie inside them.

The fate of the fortresses in Brest, Lorient, and Saint-Nazaire and of the town of Royan at the mouth of the Gironde was predetermined. They would be cut off from their supply lines, their forces largely immobile and without any contact with one another. According to the orders they were given, they were to carry out raids against the enemy so as to tie down as many of his troops as possible whilst also raising the morale of our own. That enemy would turn out to be the US VIII Corps.

The eastern troops

The total strength of the eastern troops committed to the West in 1944 amounted to approximately 80,000 men, most of whom were organised into battalions. The eastern troops at the disposal of the Seventh Army came under the command of Major-General Christoph Graf zu Stolberg-Stolberg and later of Colonel Julius Coretti. The battalions had been created by recruiting prisoners of war that had been taken in Russia and were composed of various nationalities, including Belarusians, Georgians, Cossacks, Volga Tatars, and Ossetians. While the battalions were commanded by German officers, the companies and platoons were led mostly by Baltic aristocrats or former Soviet officers. There was a strong relationship of trust and respect between the German captains and the Russian personnel. 'Who do these Russians obey?' Lieutenant-General von Choltitz once asked a young battalion commander. 'Me, General,' was the prompt reply.

Guard duties and construction tasks were the main responsibilities of the eastern battalions, and they were also entrusted with special tasks like combing through forests. They were equipped with weaponry of the kind with which they had been defeated in the East, and care always had to be taken to show respect for their sense of honour and identity. The LXXXIV Army Corps certainly did everything it could to look after these troops. They were granted leave at holiday resorts, supplied with musical instruments and chess sets, and permitted the rather administratively difficult publication of newspapers in their many languages. There did exist irreconcilable differences between some of the national groups. For example, it was impossible to accommodate Mongolians and Georgians in one holiday resort at the same time. This happened on one occasion in Valognes due to our ignorance of such tensions, and daggers were drawn as soon as the very first evening.

The combat value of the eastern troops proved to be rather low throughout the course of the invasion of Normandy. Many of them deserted, and those that remained put up such little resistance that they endangered the integrity of the front line. The reason for this is obvious. They wanted to free their motherland from Bolshevism, but they had been transferred from there to the West. The subsequent reversals on the Eastern Front had robbed them of their hopes of being able to return to their country and to their families. They thus lost confidence in the possibility of a final victory for Germany, the fate of which they would share. As a result, the initial political objective of their employment no longer applied. As Lieutenant-General Karl-Wilhelm von Schlieben once put it: 'It is too much to expect that Russians should fight for Germany in France against Americans.' The eastern troops became increasingly troubled by the thought that they might be handed over to the Bolsheviks after being captured.

One formation of eastern troops that did fight well in the combat zone of the army corps was the 439th Eastern Battalion (Major Hans Becker), which held a strongpoint at the mouth of the Vire and succeeded in finding a copy of the operational plan of the US VII Corps. Another formation that stood out was the 692nd Eastern Battalion, which belonged to Eastern Regiment Bunyachenko and fought bravely in the Forêt de Mont-Castre.

Aside from these formations, there were smaller groups of auxiliary volunteers. These troops were employed as carers and riders of horses in horse-drawn artillery and supply units, and made up approximately 10 per cent of the personnel of those units. What they achieved during the nightly withdrawal movements on congested roads was commendable. Their composure and stoicism despite stress and difficulty ought not to be overlooked.

CHAPTER 7

The daily activities of military intelligence

The primary task of German military intelligence was to obtain a picture of the intentions of the enemy forces. It collected and evaluated information pertaining to the enemy formations at the front in order to help with the making of decisions. Another important task undertaken by our military intelligence was to conceal from the enemy our own plans.

The special services that had looked after the well-being of the troops and had been so extensive in quieter times took a back seat once the invasion was underway. All that remained was the army postal service and the delivery of short reading material. The post in particular was eagerly awaited by the German soldier, its arrival always raising his spirits.

Given the multifaceted nature of military intelligence (active reconnaissance and secret communications, sabotage and insurrection, espionage in enemy territory and counterespionage against enemy military intelligence), the third general staff officer of a German formation had nothing to do with the units at the front. He knew little about and rarely needed to work with those units.

In considering the value of military intelligence, it is worth noting that every speciality relating to the conduct of warfare had been fully developed in the Prussian Army and had continued to have an effect, albeit a diminishing one, in the German Army. No other army in the nineteenth century had managed to achieve this to the same extent. The main emphasis of general staff training was placed on strategy and tactics. Other areas that dealt with the employment of military formations – like intelligence, technology, and supply – were regarded as important topics, but most officers preferred to move on from them as soon as possible. This was probably because the German soldier – confident in his training, aware of his morality, and proud of his superiority – considered such material to be of secondary importance and therefore gave it little attention.

By 1944, military intelligence personnel served in the headquarters of our formations down to divisional level. They were usually reserve officers and were passionate about their work. Sometimes lacking in proper training, they could summarise and pass on information without necessarily being able to produce tactical interpretations of that information. At regimental level and below, the work was carried out as a secondary task by orderly officers. In contrast, the Americans employed full-time personnel in military intelligence down to the battalion level, but the differences were particularly conspicuous higher up. While the third general staff officer of OB West, Lieutenant-Colonel Wilhelm Meyer-Detring, worked with nine officers, his counterpart in the American forces had 10 times as many people working for him.

At times, it was not unusual for extra work to be given to military intelligence officers. As was often said at the time: 'If no one else can or will do it, then give it to the third general staff officer!' Whenever a divisional third general staff officer failed to assert himself, he could very well find himself inundated with work that he would never have an opportunity to complete.

By and large, Hitler only ever recognised the work of our military intelligence if its findings corresponded to his own views. When there was no such correspondence, it was Hitler's opinion that the intelligence officer responsible for what he regarded as an incorrect assessment must have been fooled by the enemy or must have given in to defeatism. This circumstance was made known by the head of the OKH department Foreign Armies West, Colonel Alexis Freiherr von Roenne, to all third general staff officers in the West at a conference in the summer of 1943 at the Hotel Ambassador in Paris. Those assembled were astonished by Roenne's open and fearless criticism of Hitler. Roenne ended up being executed on 12 October 1944 in connection with the events of 20 July.

There were many officers from German divisions all over France who came to visit the front of the LXXXIV Army Corps in order to gain an impression of the situation. To make the process of briefing those officers as efficient as possible, the third orderly officer of the army corps came up with a solution. After providing a short introduction on the enemy situation, he would hand over a packet containing some material that had been captured, which might have included maps, combat reports, letters, flyers, money, 'magic balls' [magische Kugeln], ratchets, radio devices, flashlights, and compasses.

Methods of obtaining intelligence on the enemy

Prior to the invasion, there were a number of manuals and other documents of intelligence value that fell into our hands. They typically conveyed facts that were reliable, but this did not make thorough training superfluous. Our personnel still needed to apply skills relating to the interpretation of those facts, the assessment of their value, and the determination of what ought to be passed on to superior officers.

The structure of the British Army was difficult to comprehend. It had all sorts of characteristics that were foreign to us and made use of naming conventions that were steeped in tradition. The traditional body responsible for training personnel and providing replacements was the regiment, and its area of recruitment often corresponded to one of the old local counties. This type of regiment was similar in size and function to one of our replacement regiments in wartime. The tactical formation employed by the British on the battlefield was the brigade, which was the equivalent of the German field regiment of three or four battalions. The individual peacetime battalions of a British regiment, or those additional ones that had been constituted in wartime, were now allocated to different brigades or even sent to different theatres of war. However, those battalions continued to use their old designations, and the result was that multiple regimental names were to be seen in our reports for what may or may not have been one brigade that we had spotted on the battlefield. Even if we were clear about which battalions were facing us, the effort involved in deducing the division to which they belonged caused many headaches.

It was much easier to identify the American divisions. The military of the United States had seemingly appeared out of thin air, built up in accordance with the mobilisation plan of the War Department and organised similarly to our army. It had large numbers of troops and placed considerable emphasis on the concentration of artillery units. The passages that follow will deal especially with the American formations.

Insignia of the American divisions

Each American soldier wore the formation patch of his division on the upper left sleeve of his uniform, near his shoulder. This coloured insignia was also painted on vehicles. The use of shoulder sleeve insignia started in World War I when the US 81st Infantry Division introduced its formation patch in 1918, a black wildcat on a green background. It did so much for morale that the US Army soon made shoulder insignia mandatory.

Such insignia nevertheless made it easy for our military intelligence officers to gain a clear picture of the enemy situation. The division to which a prisoner of war, a man killed in action, or a destroyed or captured vehicle belonged could be identified. The insignia of the American divisions that fought against the LXXXIV Army Corps in Normandy were as follows:

- Animals or plants
    - 101st Airborne Division – screaming eagle
    - 4th Infantry Division – four stylised ivy leaves
- Geometric figures
    - V Corps – blue pentagon with white edge and radial lines
    - 5th Infantry Division – red diamond
    - 29th Infantry Division – blue and grey separated by a curved line in a circle
- Historical traditions
    - 2nd Infantry Division – head of an Indian chief
    - 35th Infantry Division – Santa Fe cross in a circle

o 79th Infantry Division – Cross of Lorraine (nickname since 1917)
- Letters
  o First Army – A
  o 82nd Airborne Division – AA (All American)
  o 90th Infantry Division – letter T bisecting the letter O (Texas-Oklahoma Division)

The postal service of the US Army

The American forces did not have army postal service numbers for the smallest units like we did. How would enemy military intelligence have interpreted numbers like 35070 or 14235b? Letters on the American side were simply stamped with something like APO 79 (Army Post Office of the 79th Infantry Division).

Code names

The code names of all the subordinate units of a division often started with the same letter. If we picked up enemy designations like Leader, Luggage, Lemon, London, or Leeboard in a certain area, we simply marked the existence of an enemy formation on our situation map and labelled it as Division L until further information revealed the number of the division.

Radio reconnaissance

Monitoring radio communications helped us to identify which enemy formations had arrived at the front. Our intelligence reconnaissance units became adept at tuning in to enemy radio traffic and determining from certain distinguishing features whether a transmission had come from an infantry or an armoured division. The number of suspected enemy formations could be confirmed to some degree by the actual strength of the enemy forces on the battlefield. If a new wave of enemy forces appeared there, our radio listening units would be ordered to focus their efforts on identifying the formations to which they belonged. Enjoying tremendous success in this regard in the combat zone of the LXXXIV Army Corps was the intelligence reconnaissance unit of the 353rd Infantry Division. This unit had gained considerable experience in southern Russia and was employed effectively by the third general staff officer of the infantry division.

Statements from prisoners of war

The American soldier had a different attitude to us on the question of being taken prisoner. He regarded a hopeless situation as a lost contest that ought quite reasonably to be given up.

All American personnel were trained on how to conduct themselves if they were captured. They understood that we treated our prisoners correctly in accordance with the Hague Convention and that they therefore need not fear refusing to testify beyond giving name and rank. And the honour of the Americans we took prisoner must be acknowledged. Most of them refrained from providing information when questioned, and that was even the case for American officers and enlisted men of German descent.

There was the occasional prisoner of war who might reveal more information. Those who were still shaken from their combat experience or from being disarmed could sometimes be tricked into talking. The interrogator would examine captured documents beforehand to learn as much as possible about orders of battle, areas of recruitment, zones of combat, boundaries between formations, code names of companies, and names of battalion and regimental commanders. He would then casually reveal his extensive knowledge to prisoners while interrogating them. Some of them were taken by surprise and, assuming he must already know everything, were willing to talk without holding anything back.

Many Americans were seized by Eisenhower's idea of a crusade against Germany. Stamps and letterheads were adorned with colourful and highly imaginative coats of arms, while propaganda was widespread, uninhibited, and psychologically influential. However, there were some Americans who expressed the opinion that their government had entered the war on the wrong side and had therefore practically rescued Bolshevism. Others, including officers, demonstrated considerable political and ideological naivety. The Anglo-Saxons also seemed rather ignorant of history and geography.

Captured documents and enemy propaganda

The Americans often disregarded the most basic principles of secrecy. Officers carried important documents into combat without considering the possibility that they might be lost. Such documents could be tactically important if they showed corps or divisional sectors or if they outlined plans for the regrouping of forces.

The war waged on the battlefield was matched by that carried out by propaganda. The main propaganda broadcaster on the Allied side was *Soldatensender Calais* ('Soldiers' Radio Calais'). Although it did not reach and therefore did not impact the German soldiers at the front, its situation reports were of interest to our headquarters staff. The measures to be taken by the LXXXIV Army Corps were sometimes predicted with astonishing accuracy. Such predictions were often possible due to certain tactical necessities in the combat zone, but it clearly indicated that the broadcaster had a military specialist in its employ. Its conjectures on what Choltitz would do next were occasionally so spot-on that he once responded to a query by Hausser regarding his intentions as follows: 'You need only listen to *Soldatensender Calais!*' This type of coverage, whereby predictions were made on our intentions, was ceased after a few weeks. It can be presumed that the enemy had attempted to dissuade us from making the best decisions by announcing them beforehand, but he probably soon realised that this tactic did not work.

Propaganda delivered by the enemy to the front itself came in the form of *Nachrichten für die Truppe* ('News for the Troops'). This richly illustrated and flawlessly printed leaflet was produced in large numbers and dropped by enemy aircraft over our positions. Its written style was perfectly geared towards the ordinary German soldier, and its coverage of Allied successes was underlined with maps, photos, and photo montages. Several details were included which could be easily verified by our men, the psychological objective of which was to convince them that the entire text was true. There were special issues which focused on certain sectors of the front, with the destruction of the 709th Infantry Division at Cherbourg, for example, being announced under the headline 'Das Schicksal einer Division' ('The Fate of a Division'). The primitive treatment of some historical and cultural themes came to the fore, with Prussia in particular being represented with cliches, but the topicality of the leaflet testified to a state of good cooperation between enemy intelligence and enemy propaganda and to the employment of the most modern technological achievements in the most extravagant way possible.

It can be concluded that the degree of success of enemy propaganda did not correspond to the relentlessness with which it was produced and distributed. There were various reasons for this clear failure. Even if *Nachrichten für die Truppe* reported some events correctly, it smelled of propaganda from the outset. Our men at the front knew that their families and their Fatherland stood behind them, that the Allied bombing of our cities was not restricted to military targets, and that the enemy had demanded of us no less than unconditional surrender. They were immune to being worn down by words and were eager to hold out for peace on favourable terms. There was a big difference between, on the one hand, rejecting the prevailing system and wanting to bring about change with force from within and, on the other, being willing to desert one's post or even to collaborate with the BBC. In every army in the world, desertion from one's post or collaboration with the enemy is morally wrong.

German propaganda and the French population

Our propaganda dealt with a number of themes. It addressed Western and Christian cultural awareness of the fact that the Lend-Lease policies of the West would serve only to preserve Bolshevism, appealed to the common blood shared by many Germans and Americans, invoked the concern of Americans that they were being killed or mutilated for nothing more than political or economic interests, played on the fears of Americans that they were losing their jobs at home and that they were being exploited by wartime profiteers, and published extracts from captured correspondence that expressed combat fatigue. The success of our propaganda was as limited as that of the enemy, or perhaps more so given that he was fully confident that the outcome of the war would be decided in his favour. As one American prisoner of war put it: 'Propaganda is only really taken seriously by propagandists.'

We enjoyed a good relationship with the French population on the Cotentin Peninsula. The Norman peasants were pedestrian yet friendly, and they got by perfectly well during the period of the occupation. They soon welcomed the presence of the German soldiers. Aside from the fact that we placed few demands on accommodation and made our horse-drawn units available to assist with the harvest, our men demonstrated good manners, paid well for everything, and treated women and girls even more chivalrously than the French themselves did. The peasants often remarked on the correctness of our behaviour and drew comparisons with how poorly French troops had conducted themselves during peacetime manoeuvres in the area. It should also be pointed out that many French mayors stood up for German soldiers who had been taken prisoner while the invasion was underway. They risked their own necks in so doing, for it was dangerous in 1944 to even be suspected of collaboration. The situation was similar in the Channel Islands at a later stage. Several residents sent letters to prison camps in England in support of former occupation personnel.

A number of reports delivered to us by members of the French Militia, led by Joseph Darnand, from areas occupied by the enemy to the south of Cherbourg were of interest to us. It appeared as if any understanding between the French population and the American liberators was short-lived. Reasons for this included the heavy casualties inflicted on civilians by the Allied bombing of small towns, the enforced introduction of a new yet widely distrusted currency, the restrictions – apparently on sanitary grounds – on interactions between American troops and French civilians, the tactless judgement of French customs whenever such interactions took place, and the primitive cultural perspectives of many Allied soldiers.

The evening reports

The work of the intelligence section of the army corps was summarised each day in an evening report. An excerpt from such a report, the structure of which was standardised, from the middle of July 1944 is presented below. It provided an appraisal of the situation at that time:

(a) [Our operational situation in keywords.]
(b) Appearing in the combat zone:
 On the US Third Army (Patton), see the captured document 'Orders for the employment of the 4th Infantry Division in the Normandy beachhead'.
(c) Confirmed:
 The US 2nd Infantry Division has been identified from the dead of the US 28th Infantry Regiment and from the presence of the Army Post Office of the US 2nd Infantry Division on Hill 192 by the N172 highway (US V Corps). The US 82nd Airborne Division has not been seen since 10 July. Has it been relieved?
(d) Enemy aerial activity:
 Many light bombs with time fuses were dropped. Photoflash bombs were dropped as well on the night of 14/15 July after enemy aerial reconnaissance had been conducted during the day in the Lessay–Périers area.
(e) Prisoners of war:
 A total of 235 enemy troops belonging to the US 90th Infantry Division (mostly the III Battalion of the US 357th Infantry Regiment) have been captured since 4 July on Hill 42, east of Forêt de Mont-Castre. Ten crewmen from two Flying Fortresses that came down to the north of Marigny have been handed over to the Luftwaffe. The search for the remaining crewmen is underway.
(f) Captured:
 3 heavy machine guns, 5 light machine guns, 3 medium mortars, 43 submachine guns, 5 radio sets, and 1 hedge cutting machine.
(g) Destroyed:
 6 Sherman tanks destroyed by our anti-tank guns and rocket launchers, 4 tanks rendered immobile, and 3 fighter-bombers shot down by our army anti-aircraft guns.

(h) Artillery situation:
Heavy artillery fire during the day against our observation posts in the Lessay–Périers area. Farmsteads, for the first time, have also been targeted. Decreased battery fire on the northern front, in the sector of the US XIX Corps. Isolated rounds fired by new batteries in the vicinity of La Haye-du-Puits and Sainteny. Is this adjustment fire?

(i) Radio reconnaissance:
According to our radio reconnaissance, the radio frequency of the US 3rd Armored Division is 2201 kilohertz. There has been radio silence in the area to the south of Carentan and Isigny since 1000 hours.

(j) Propaganda:
1. Enemy propaganda
Leaflets have been dropped informing Germanised Poles that they will be offered special permits. The same has been offered to eastern troops via Russian-language leaflets that have been dropped in the combat zone of Eastern Regiment Bunyachenko. An enemy loudspeaker vehicle has been driven away by our artillery zone fire.

2. Our propaganda
'Stalin or your wife' leaflets distributed by the 649th Propaganda Rocket Launcher Platoon. The focus of the special services for our troops must be improved delivery of post, newspapers, and short reading matter (Reclam). For days, the only German-language material the troops have received is the enemy publication *Nachrichten für die Truppe*. The distribution of our own material from ration distribution points has been proposed. A storage area for us at the propaganda strongpoint in Barenton is not possible.

(k) Assessment of the enemy situation:
The enemy is concentrating his artillery units and has shifted his divisional sectors opposite the central part of the front of the army corps in order to create points of main effort for his attack. The US 83rd Infantry Division has been moved to this area. Our ground reconnaissance has spotted heavy traffic proceeding

through Baupte towards the south-east, while our spy reports tell us that further traffic is flowing over the dam in La Sangsutier towards the south. Enemy aerial reconnaissance north-east of Périers is indicative of preparations for an attack. The presumed objective of the enemy is to break through Périers and to advance from the area of Saint-Lô towards Coutances and the west coast of the Cotentin Peninsula.

Given Eisenhower's aversion to conducting operations on Sundays, the attack will probably commence on Monday.

I telephoned the third general staff officer of the Seventh Army, Lieutenant-Colonel Vorwerk, myself, and a radio message was sent when we moved out at 2040 hours.

Third General Staff Officer
LXXXIV Army Corps
Major Hayn

Formations mentioned in the text

German formations

A. Corps and armies
I SS Panzer Corps
II SS Panzer Corps
II Parachute Corps
XXV Army Corps
XXXXVII Panzer Corps
LXXIV Army Corps
LXXX Army Corps
LXXXI Army Corps
LXXXIV Army Corps
LXXXVI Army Corps
Panzer Group West (Fifth Panzer Army)
Panzer Group Eberbach

B. Divisions
3rd Parachute Division
5th Parachute Division
16th Luftwaffe Field Division
77th Infantry Division
84th Infantry Division
89th Infantry Division
91st Air Landing Division

158th Infantry Division
243rd Infantry Division
265th Infantry Division
266th Infantry Division
271st Infantry Division
272nd Grenadier Division
275th Infantry Division
276th Infantry Division
277th Infantry Division
319th Infantry Division
326th Infantry Division
331st Infantry Division
343rd Grenadier Division
346th Infantry Division
352nd Infantry Division
353rd Infantry Division
363rd Infantry Division
708th Infantry Division
709th Infantry Division
711th Infantry Division
716th Infantry Division
Blocking Force Kortüm
Blocking Force Heckel
1st SS Panzer Division Leibstandarte SS Adolf Hitler
2nd SS Panzer Division Das Reich
2nd Panzer Division
9th Panzer Division
9th SS Panzer Division Hohenstaufen
10th SS Panzer Division Frundsberg
12th SS Panzer Division Hitlerjugend
21st Panzer Division
116th Panzer Division
Panzer Lehr Division
17th SS Panzer Grenadier Division Götz von Berlichingen

C. Regiments and brigades, excluding those mentioned in the context of their parent divisions

1st Motorised Security Regiment
6th Parachute Regiment
7th Werfer Brigade
8th Werfer Brigade
9th Werfer Brigade
25th Motorised Flak Regiment
30th Mobile Brigade
393rd Assault Gun Brigade
521st Security Regiment
752nd Infantry Regiment
Eastern Regiment Bunyachenko

D. Battalions, excluding those mentioned in the context of their parent regiments

Assault battalion of the Seventh Army
17th Machine Gun Battalion
439th Eastern Battalion
635th Eastern Battalion
639th Eastern Battalion
692nd Eastern Battalion
795th Georgian Battalion
797th Georgian Battalion

American formations

A. Corps

V Corps
VII Corps
VIII Corps
XII Corps
XV Corps
XIX Corps
XX Corps

B. Divisions

1st Infantry Division
2nd Infantry Division
4th Infantry Division
5th Infantry Division
8th Infantry Division
9th Infantry Division
29th Infantry Division
30th Infantry Division
35th Infantry Division
79th Infantry Division
80th Infantry Division
82nd Airborne Division
83rd Infantry Division
90th Infantry Division
101st Airborne Division
2nd Armored Division
3rd Armored Division
4th Armored Division
6th Armored Division
8th Armored Division
French 2nd Armored Division

British formations

A. Corps

I Corps
Canadian II Corps
VIII Corps
XXX Corps

B. Divisions

Canadian 2nd Infantry Division
Canadian 3rd Infantry Division
3rd Infantry Division

6th Airborne Division
7th Infantry Division
43rd (Wessex) Infantry Division
50th (Northumbrian) Infantry Division
51st (Highland) Infantry Division
Polish 1st Armoured Division
Canadian 4th Armoured Division
7th Armoured Division
79th Armoured Division

References

Published sources

American Forces in Action Series, Historical Division, War Department, Washington D.C. *Omaha Beachhead* (1945), *St-Lo* (1946), *Utah Beach to Cherbourg* (1947).

Choltitz, Dietrich von. *Soldat unter Soldaten: Die deutsche Armee im Frieden und im Krieg.* Zurich: Europa Verlag, 1951.

Eisenhower, Dwight D. *Invasion: General Eisenhowers eigener Kriegsbericht.* Hamburg: J. P. Toth Verlag, 1949.

Montgomery, B. L. *Von El Alamein zum Sangro – Von der Normandie zur Ostsee.* Hamburg: J. P. Toth Verlag, 1949.

Speidel, Hans. *Invasion 1944: Ein Beitrag zu Rommels und des Reiches Schicksal.* Tübingen: Rainer Wunderlich Verlag Hermann Leins, 1949.

Stjernfelt, Bertil. *Alarm i Atlantvallen.* Stockholm: Hörsta Förlag, 1953.

Tippelskirch, Kurt von. *Geschichte des zweiten Weltkrieges.* Bonn: Athenäum-Verlag, 1951.

Unpublished sources

Author's notes.

Reports written by German generals while held in captivity in England and Oberursel in 1945 and 1946 (see foreword).

War diary of OB West.

The maps are drawn by Herbert Sielaff, Hamburg, and are based on sketches by the author.

Index

aerial superiority of Allies, 2, 4, 6, 8, 21–22, 25, 27–28, 30, 37, 39, 45, 61, 66, 91, 107, 113–114, 122, 133–134, 138, 142
Alençon, 24, 96, 98, 106, 112, 114–116
Amiens, 2, 124
area bombing, 72, 78, 118, 139
Argentan, 96, 110, 112–114, 116, 119, 121, 124–125, 129
Aufseß, Hugo Freiherr von, 23, 81
Avignon, 11, 102
Avranches, 40, 57, 65, 85, 88, 91–92, 98–99, 102, 106–108, 111–113, 136

Bacherer, Rudolf, 54–55, 99–101
Bailleul, 123–124
Balleroy, 48, 70, 80
Barenton, 95, 113, 159
Barneville, 49, 54, 65
Bayerlein, Fritz, 24, 37, 77
Bayeux, 37, 44, 70, 79
Bénouville, 8, 19
Bérigny, 79, 83
Bittrich, Wilhelm, 95, 121
Bourguébus, 68, 109
box bombing tactics, 109, 111, 138–139
Brécy, 101–102
Bretteville, 73, 111
Bricquebec, 54, 58
Brieux, 122, 124
British armed forces

Armies
  Second, 93, 117
  Eighth, 21
Corps
  I, 20, 70
  VIII, 69, 78
  XXX, 44
Infantry Divisions
  3rd, 20
  43rd (Wessex), 96
  50th (Northumbrian), 21, 37
  51st (Highland), 21
organisation of, 151–152

Cabourg, 26, 68
Caen, 2, 5, 8, 19–21, 24, 26–28, 30, 35, 37–38, 40, 43, 67, 69–70, 78–79, 82, 91, 93–94, 96, 104, 108–111, 115, 118, 138, 140
Canadian armed forces
  Armies
    First, 93, 96, 109
  Armoured Divisions
    4th, 111, 119
  conduct of battle of, 109
  Infantry Divisions
    3rd, 20, 72
Canal de Vire et Taute, 56, 73, 75–76
Canisy, 83, 85
Carentan, 4–5, 8–9, 15, 29, 35, 41, 45–46, 48–49, 64, 75–76, 91, 140, 159

Caumont, 48, 67, 69–70, 73, 80, 83, 139
Cavigny, 56, 73, 76
Cérences, 23, 87–88, 90
Chambois, 98, 122, 124, 126, 128–130
Champ-du-Boult, 94, 108
Chênedollé, 115–116
Cherbourg, 2, 10, 30–31, 42–44, 46, 54, 56, 64, 91, 143, 157
   battle of, 48–51, 53, 57–63, 65, 144, 156
Choltitz, Dietrich von, 56, 62, 73, 85, 87–88, 90, 99, 145, 147, 155
   career of, 56–57
Colleville, 9, 81
Collins, J. Lawton, 58, 63
Condé, 96, 117
Coutances, 23, 56, 64, 85, 160
Criegern, Friedrich von, xi, 1, 12, 46–47, 49–50, 87, 108

D-Day, vii, 1–10, 12–31, 34, 40, 44, 76, 91, 115
   Allied airborne landings on, 4–6, 9, 15–18, 23, 31
   Allied seaborne landings on, 5–6, 8–9, 13, 15, 17, 26, 31
   German defensive preparations prior to, 12, 58, 60, 133, 142
Dietrich, Sepp, 24, 94
Domfront, 95, 113, 116
Doville, 51, 55

Eberbach, Heinrich, xi, 94, 113, 121
Eisenhower, Dwight D., 154, 160
Elfeldt, Otto, 88, 94, 108, 122, 124, 129

Fahrmbacher, Wilhelm, 48–50, 56
Falaise, 93, 96, 109, 111–112, 114, 117–118, 121, 124
Falaise pocket, vii, xi, 70, 97, 114, 116, 118–119, 121–122, 124–126, 128–130, 145

Falley, Wilhelm, 7–8
Feuchtinger, Edgar, 19–20, 24
Flers, 115–116
Forêt de Cerisy, 48, 69, 79
Forêt de Gouffern, 121, 125
Forêt de Mont-Castre, 72–73, 148, 158
fortresses, 146–147
French population, 12, 26, 55, 98, 157
French Resistance, 4, 6, 146
Funck, Hans Freiherr von, 82, 94

German armed forces
   Air Landing Divisions
      91st, 7–8, 16, 33, 42, 49, 51, 58, 82, 90
   Armies
      Seventh, passim
      Fifteenth, 29, 41, 111
   Army Coastal Artillery Regiment Triepel, 34, 41
   Army Coastal Battery Azeville, 36, 41
   Army Corps
      XXV, 48, 146
      LXXIV, 29, 40, 115, 124, 146
      LXXXI, 26, 29, 95, 113, 116
      LXXXIV, passim
      LXXXVI, 68, 115
   Army Field Gun Battery Merville, 8, 26, 36
   Army Group B, 7, 9, 19, 28, 39–40, 42, 49, 61, 82, 112–113, 115, 141–142
   Army Group D, 112, 141–142
   Battle Group Heinz, 40, 75, 86, 90
   Battle Group Rohrbach, 57–58
   conduct of battle of, 72–73, 133–136
   eastern battalions, 43, 69, 76, 147–148, 159
   Eastern Regiment Bunyachenko, 72, 148, 159

INDEX • 171

Grenadier Regiments
  919th, 60
  922nd, 50
  941st, 82, 86
  957th, 90
  984th, 109
Infantry Divisions
  77th, 40, 42, 49, 51–54, 68–69, 72, 99, 146
  84th, 104, 116, 130
  89th, 109, 111, 115
  243rd, 49–51, 55, 62, 69, 86–87, 90
  265th, 40, 69
  275th, 40, 69, 75, 85–86, 146
  319th, 28, 51, 143, 146
  326th, 82, 115, 117
  331st, 115–116
  346th, 68, 115
  352nd, 8–9, 12–13, 22, 35, 43, 69, 80, 85, 106
  353rd, 55–56, 65–66, 69, 73, 75, 82–83, 86, 90, 94, 108–109, 116, 126–127, 129, 146, 154
  363rd, 90, 104, 108, 116, 124–125
  708th, 95, 113, 116
  709th, 5, 34–35, 42, 49–50, 63, 156
  711th, 26, 68, 115
  716th, 4–5, 20, 22–23, 27
Infantry Regiments
  726th, 24, 35
  915th, 8, 15, 23, 35
  919th, 9, 17–18, 29, 34, 42, 62
Luftwaffe, 22, 24, 60, 62, 141, 143, 158
  inferiority or absence of, 10, 21, 27, 44, 48, 61, 100, 140
Luftwaffe Field Divisions
  16th, 70, 78, 115
Luftwaffe signal centre in Caen, 8, 21

Mobile Brigades
  30th, 23, 35, 69, 76, 81
morale of, viii, 2, 68, 88, 124, 147, 149
Naval Coastal Battery Hamburg, 36, 61
Naval Coastal Battery Longues, 23, 36
Naval Coastal Battery Saint-Marcouf, 23, 33–34, 36
OB West (German Army Command in the West), 39, 43, 50, 64, 86, 96, 98–99, 103, 112, 114, 119, 141, 143, 150
OKW (High Command of the Wehrmacht), 31, 39, 49–50, 94, 112–113, 142, 144, 146
  assumes Normandy landings were merely diversionary, 28–29, 41, 65, 143
  interferes in conduct of operations, 143, 145
  organisation of, 68, 133, 141–144, 146–147
Panzer Armies
  Fifth, 94, 98, 104, 111, 115, 121
Panzer Corps
  XXXXVII, 69, 82, 94, 96, 103, 106, 116, 124, 129
  LVIII, 116
  LXXVI, 56
Panzer Divisions
  2nd, 82, 86, 94, 106–107, 116, 128–129
  9th, 95, 113–114, 116
  21st, 19–20, 24, 37, 69–70, 78, 114–115
  116th, 82, 90, 94–95, 106, 116, 121, 128–129
Panzer Group Eberbach, 94, 96, 113–114, 128

Panzer Group West, 39, 68, 70, 94
Panzer Lehr Division, 24, 37, 69, 77–78, 81, 85, 90, 106, 116
Parachute Corps
  II, 39, 69, 79, 83, 94, 106, 108–109, 116–117, 124, 126
Parachute Divisions
  3rd, 40, 48, 69, 79–80, 82, 108, 116, 126, 128, 146
  5th, 72, 83, 90, 116, 146
Parachute Regiments
  6th, 16, 45–46, 69, 90
  15th, 72, 83
signals and communications of, 8, 10, 20, 22, 24–25, 37, 49–50, 60, 62, 87, 98–99, 141, 149, 153–154
SS Panzer Corps
  I, 24, 69, 94, 115
  II, 70, 94–95, 98, 121–122, 125, 130, 144
SS Panzer Divisions
  1st (Leibstandarte SS Adolf Hitler), 78, 94, 106, 116, 122, 129
  2nd (Das Reich), 69, 76–77, 87, 90, 94, 106–107, 116, 122
  9th (Hohenstaufen), 70, 95, 116
  10th (Frundsberg), 70, 95, 116
  12th (Hitlerjugend), 24, 37, 69–70, 72, 109, 115, 118, 128
SS Panzer Grenadier Divisions
  17th (Götz von Berlichingen), 41, 46, 48, 69, 75, 90, 106, 116, 140
supply problems or shortages of, 19, 22, 41, 78, 88, 98, 100, 114, 137, 147
traffic problems experienced by, 2, 5, 22, 116–117, 122–123, 136, 148
Werfer Brigades
  7th, 68
  8th, 56, 121
  9th, 121

German military intelligence, vii–ix, 6, 10, 25, 75, 101–102, 119, 140–141, 145, 149–154, 158
Gersdorff, Rudolf-Christoph Freiherr von, xi, 88, 128–129, 145
Gourfaleur, 83, 108
Graignes, 56, 73, 76
Granville, 56, 146
Green Line, 88, 90

Hausser, Paul, viii, 70, 128–129, 155
  career and qualities of, 144–145
Hayn, Friedrich, vii–viii, xi, 1, 4–5, 21, 25–26, 37, 44, 47–48, 73, 101–103, 124, 130–131, 160
Hellmich, Heinz, 7, 51
Hill 192, 79, 158
Hitler, Adolf, vii, 11, 29, 48, 51, 61, 81, 98, 103–104, 143–145, 150

Isigny, 4, 41, 43, 159

Keil, Günther, xi, 9, 60
Kluge, Günther von, 86, 96, 103–104, 111, 113, 119
Kraiß, Dietrich, 7, 43, 106
Kuntzen, Adolf-Friedrich, 29, 95

La Haye-du-Puits, 49, 53, 72–73, 159
La-Lande-Vaumont, 96, 108
La Meauffe, 56, 80
landing craft, 12, 63
La Roche-Guyon, 19, 141
Le Dézert, 73, 76–77
Le Ham, 42, 50
Le Havre, 31, 65
Le Mans, 19, 37, 93, 96, 98, 112, 144
Lessay, 22–23, 40, 83, 139, 158–159
Lisieux, 79, 121–122
London, 50, 67
Lorient, 40, 147

Lüttwitz, Heinrich Freiherr von, 94, 129

Macon, Robert C., 100–101
Mahlmann, Paul, xi, 65, 73, 126
Marcks, Erich, 1–2, 4, 8, 12, 19–20, 22–23, 40, 46, 57–58, 81
  death of, 39, 47–48
  life and career of, 10–12
Marigny, 75, 83, 108, 158
Mayenne, 113, 116
Meindl, Eugen, 39, 79, 83, 94
Metz, 2, 112
Meulles, 115, 122
Meyer-Detring, Wilhelm, xi, 43, 150
Model, Walter, 96, 119
Moissy, 126, 129
Montabard, 123, 125
Mont Castre, 72–73
Montebourg, 19, 41–42, 57–58
Montgomery, Bernard, 21, 24, 29, 67, 70, 79, 93, 125
Mont-Ormel, 124, 126
Mont Pinçon, 96, 117
Mortain, 93–96, 103, 111, 113, 116
  panzer counter-attack at, 94–96, 102–104, 106–108, 111, 114–115, 143
Mulberry harbours, 63, 67

Nachrichten für die Truppe, 63, 155–156, 159
Nettuno, 56–57

Paris, 2, 11, 57, 106–107, 112, 141, 150
Patton, George S., 67, 93, 158
Pemsel, Max, 88, 139, 145
Percy, 86, 88, 90
Périers, 9, 46–47, 56, 66, 75, 83, 139, 158–160
Pierrefitte, 119, 124

Polish 1st Armoured Division, 111, 119, 125, 129
Pont-Hébert, 69, 75–77, 80
Pont-l'Abbé, 5, 16, 42
Portbail, 51, 55, 64
Port-en-Bessin, 9, 35
Prairies Marécageuses, 51, 56, 69
Prairies Marécageuses de Gorges, 56, 73, 75
Putanges, 115, 117, 119

Quinéville, 41–42, 50, 57

Ranville, 4–5, 8, 19
Rennes, 1, 7, 90
Riva-Bella, 9, 26
Rivers
  Aire, 48, 79
  Aure, 4, 35, 69
  Dives, 5, 39, 79, 93, 116–117, 119, 121–123, 125, 130
  Douve, 4, 44–45, 51, 58
  Laison, 96, 111–112, 117
  Loire, 2, 41, 93, 95
  Merderet, 4–5, 16, 40, 42, 44
  Odon, 69–70, 117
  Orne, 4–5, 8, 19–20, 24, 26, 28, 39, 67, 69–70, 79, 93, 96, 115–118
  Rance, 99–100
  Sée, 94, 106
  Seine, 2, 10, 93, 102, 123, 141
  Sienne, 85–86, 90
  Varenne, 95, 116
  Vire, 37, 39, 41, 43, 47, 56, 65, 69, 73, 75–77, 79, 81, 83, 85, 116, 148
Rommel, Erwin, 7, 21, 37, 40, 50, 61, 79, 133, 141–142, 144
Rônai, 122, 124
Rouen, 2, 26, 29, 95, 104, 122
Royan, 95, 147
Rundstedt, Gerd von, 141–142

Sainte-Mère-Église, 3, 5, 16–17, 19, 23, 33
Sainteny, 56, 73, 75, 159
Saint-Germain-de-Varreville, 5, 18
Saint-Jean-de-Bois, 104, 116
Saint-Jean-de-Daye, 75–76
Saint-Lambert, 98, 122, 125–126, 128–129
Saint-Laurent-sur-Mer, 13, 81
Saint-Lô, 1, 9, 30, 41, 43, 47–48, 69, 73–74, 76, 79–83, 86, 91, 139, 160
Saint-Lô-d'Ourville, 53, 56
Saint-Malo, 4, 95, 99, 146
Saint-Nazaire, 40, 147
Saint-Pois, 94, 102
Saint-Sauveur-le-Vicomte, 49, 51, 85
Schimpf, Richard, 80, 126
Schlieben, Karl-Wilhelm von, 7, 42, 50, 57–58, 61–63, 148
Schmettow, Rudolf Graf von, 7, 28
Schweppenburg, Leo Freiherr Geyr von, 39, 94
Soldatensender Calais, 123, 155
Sourdeval, 88, 108, 111, 116
Stegmann, Rudolf, 40, 51, 53–54
Straube, Erich, 29–30

terrain in Normandy, 60, 66–67, 72, 106, 114, 133–135
  effectiveness of tanks in, 136–137
Thury-Harcourt, 39, 115
Tilly, 37, 39, 48, 70, 109
Tilly-sur-Seulles, 37, 69, 77
Tinchebray, 96, 104, 108, 116–117
Tournai, 125–126, 130
Troarn, 26, 68, 79, 115
Trun, 98, 121–122, 124–125, 128
Turqueville, 34–35

US armed forces
  Airborne Divisions
    82nd, 5, 15–16, 18, 42, 51, 54, 73, 153, 158
    101st, 5, 17–18, 45, 152
  Air Forces
    Eighth, 51, 78, 138
    Ninth, 78, 138
  Armies
    First, 65, 72, 82, 89, 93, 104, 153
    Third, 67, 93, 95, 103, 112, 122, 158
  Armored Divisions
    2nd, 77, 85
    3rd, 49, 76, 91, 159
    4th, 90–91, 99
    conduct of battle of, 60, 66–68, 134, 136–138
  Corps
    V, 27, 44, 48, 79, 93, 96, 152, 158
    VII, 18, 41, 44, 53, 58, 73, 77, 85, 91, 93, 107, 148
    VIII, 85, 91, 93, 147
    XV, 93, 96, 112–113
    XIX, 75, 77, 80, 93, 159
  Infantry Divisions
    1st, 13, 35, 73
    2nd, 152, 158
    4th, 17, 19, 34–35, 41, 58, 91, 152, 158
    8th, 73, 91
    9th, 42, 49, 53, 58, 61, 77, 91
    29th, 13, 81, 152
    30th, 75–77
    79th, 58, 91, 153
    83rd, 73, 91, 100, 159
    90th, 42, 72, 77, 91, 121, 125, 128, 131, 153, 158
  Infantry Regiments
    8th, 19
    12th, 41
    16th, 13
    26th, 37
    28th, 158
    39th, 53, 77
    47th, 55
    116th, 13

    120th, 76
    137th, 80
    177th, 107
    357th, 158
    morale of, viii, 18, 136, 152
    Parachute Infantry Regiments
        502nd, 34, 45
        505th, 5, 17
    signals and communications of, 140–141
US military intelligence, 150, 153
US prisoners of war, 13, 15, 23, 37, 73, 76, 108, 154–155, 157–158

Valognes, 5, 7, 9–10, 40, 50, 58, 148
Vidouville, 80, 83
Viebig, Hasso, 1, 9, 44, 124
Vierville, 9, 19, 35
Villedieu, 90, 102, 123, 125
Villers-Bocage, 48, 69–70
Vimoutiers, 98, 115, 121, 130
Vire, 93–94, 104, 108, 111, 116

Wisch, Theodor, 78, 94